A WOMAN
OF GREAT COURAGE

. . . Harriet Tubman explained her decision to
run the risk of going North alone in these words:
"I had reasoned this out in my mind; there was
one of two things I had a *right* to, liberty or
death; if I could not have one, I would have the
other; for no man should take me alive; I should
fight for my liberty as long as my strength lasted,
and when the time came for me to go, the Lord
would let them take me."

"**An unusually fine biography. . . . This
sensitive, skillfully narrated account of
Harriet Tubman's life and dedicated work,
more than other books on the subject,
paints a lifelike and poignant portrait of
the indomitable woman whose faith in
God and belief in freedom sustained her
through years of daily risks, physical hard-
ships, and emotional stress.**"
—*A.L.A. Booklist*

"**Hers is one of the great stories of that
tragic era. Ann Petry tells it with insight,
style and a fine narrative skill. . . .**"
—*The New York Times*

HARRIET TUBMAN

Conductor on the
Underground Railroad

by ANN PETRY

AN ARCHWAY PAPERBACK
Published by POCKET BOOKS
New York   London   Toronto   Sydney   Tokyo

The excerpt from *John Brown's Body* by Stephen
Vincent Benét, published by Rinehart & Com-
pany, copyright 1927, 1928 by Stephen Vincent
Benét is reprinted by permission.

An Archway Paperback published by
POCKET BOOKS, a division of Simon & Schuster Inc.
1230 Avenue of the Americas, New York, N.Y. 10020

Published by arrangement with Thomas Y. Crowell Company, Publishers
Library of Congress Catalog Card Number: 55-9215

ISBN: 0-671-50442-8

First Pocket Books printing February 1971

16   15   14   13   12   11

AN ARCHWAY PAPERBACK and colophon are
registered trademarks of Simon & Schuster Inc.

Printed in the U.S.A.

IL 7+

This book is for
Elisabeth Ann Petry

Contents

"... you fought for the single dream
   of a man unchained
And God's great chariot rolling."
STEPHEN VINCENT BENÉT
John Brown's Body

HARRIET TUBMAN

1. The Quarter

CHESAPEAKE BAY forms the western boundary of the section of Maryland which is sometimes called Tidewater Maryland, sometimes called the Eastern Shore. Here there are so many coves and creeks, rivers and small streams, that the land areas are little more than heads or necks of land, almost surrounded by water.

In these streams the ebb and flow of the tide is visible for miles inland—hence the name Tidewater Maryland.

In 1820, much of the Eastern Shore was heavily wooded. The streams were filled with fish. Game birds—wild duck and snipe—abounded in all of the coves and marshes. It could truly be said that every plantation thereabout "at its garden gate, has an oyster-bed, a fishing-bar, and a ducking blind."

The plantation that belonged to Edward Brodas, in Dorchester County, was typical of this section of Maryland, for one of its land boundaries was a river—the Big Buckwater River. It was more or less isolated. The nearest village, Bucktown, was little more than a settlement composed of post office, church, crossroads store, and eight or ten dwelling houses.

There was an air of leisure about the planter's

1

life here. Fishing and hunting were an integral part of it, just as it had been part of the life of the Indians, who had practically disappeared from the Eastern Shore by 1750.

The house in which Edward Brodas lived was very large. There had to be room for his friends, his relatives, as well as his family. Visitors came from long distances, and so usually stayed a month or two before undertaking the journey back home. There were extra rooms for travelers, who carried the proper letters of introduction, because inns and taverns offered uncertain lodging for the night.

Edward Brodas was known as the Master to his Negro slaves. His house, which the slaves called the Big House, stood near a country road. The kitchen was a small detached building in the rear, known as the cookhouse. Not too far away from the Big House were the stables, where the riding horses and the carriage horses, the grooms and the hostlers were housed. Close to the stables were the kitchen gardens and the cutting gardens. Beyond these lay the orchards and the barns for the work horses and cows and mules.

The Big House, the cookhouse, the stables, formed a complete unit. Beyond this lay the fields, the clear cultivated land bordered by the forest.

Out of sight of the Big House, but not quite out of hearing, was the "quarter" where the slaves lived.

The quarter consisted of a group of one-room, windowless cabins. They were built of logs that had been cut from the nearby forests. The chinks were filled with mud. These roughhewn logs were filled with sap, and as they dried out, the wood contracting and expanding with changes in temperature, the roofs sagged, the walls buckled. The narrow clay-daubed chimneys leaned as though some unseen pressure were forcing them over. Seen from a distance, these sway-backed cabins seemed to huddle together as though for protection. The fact that they were exactly alike, that they were surrounded by the same barren hard-packed earth, furthered the illusion.

The cabins were exactly alike inside, too. There was a crude fireplace with one or two black iron pots standing in front of it. The hearth was merely a continuation of the dirt floor. When the wind blew hard, smoke came down the chimney, into the room, in puffs, so that the walls were smoke-darkened. Even in summer there was a characteristic smoky smell in the cabins.

The fireplace not only provided heat in winter, it was the source of light, and it was used for cooking. Piles of old worn-out blankets served as beds. There were no chairs; so the occupants of the cabins either squatted in front of the fire or sat on the floor. In the middle of the dirt floor there was a large, fairly deep hole covered over with loose boards. This was the potato hole, where sweet potatoes were stored in winter to protect them from the frost.

Harriet Greene, who was usually called Old Rit, and her husband, Benjamin Ross, both slaves, lived in one of these windowless cabins, in the quarter, on the Brodas plantation. They had several children, some of whom still lived with them. The older children were "hired out" by the master, Edward Brodas, to farmers who needed slave labor but who could not afford to buy slaves.

In 1820, Old Rit had another baby. There was no record made of the date of the birth of this child, because neither Old Rit nor her husband, Ben, could read or write.

Like most people who live close to the land, and who have neither clock nor calendar, they measured time by the sun, dividing it roughly into sunup, sunhigh, sundown. The year was not divided by months but by the seasons. It was separated into Seedtime, Cotton Blossomtime, Harvest, Christmas. One year was distinguished from another by its happenings, its big, memorable occurrences— the year of the big storm, the year of the early frost, or the long drought, the year the old master died, the year the young master was born.

Old Rit and Ben decided that they would call this new baby Araminta, a name that would be ultimately shortened to Minta or Minty. This would be her basket name or pet name, and would be used until she grew older. Then they would call her Harriet. That year would be separated from the others by referring to it as "the year Minty was born."

News, good or bad, traveled swiftly through the quarter. All the slaves knew that Old Rit had another baby. That night they left their own cabins, moving like shadows, pausing now and then to listen, always expecting to hear the sound of hoof-beats, loud and furious, along the road, a sound that meant the patrollers were hunting another runaway. Only they added an extra syllable to the word, making it "patteroller." Then, moving quietly, quickly, they slipped inside Ben's cabin, to look at the new baby.

They arrived in groups, two or three at a time, and stood looking down at the baby. It was a girl. They already knew that, but they asked whether it was a boy or a girl out of politeness; and asked what her name would be, though they knew that, too.

Girls were not worth much, and Old Rit already had a passel of children, but they did not say this. They suggested tactfully that Old Rit had better see to it that this new girl baby was trained as a cook or a weaver or a seamstress. Perhaps she could take care of children, be a child's nurse. That way she would never become a common field hand.

They admired the baby, briefly. They asked after the mother's health, and then lingered on, squatting down in front of the open fire, talking. The talk around the fire was about the new overseer, about the corn crop, about the weather, but it ended with the subject of freedom—just as it always did.

The bold ones, young, strong, said freedom lay to the North, and one could obtain it if one could but get there. A hush fell over the cabin, an uneasiness entered the room. It seemed to reach the sleeping children, huddled on the old blankets in the corner, for they stirred in their sleep.

They were all silent for a moment, remembering the ragged, half-starved runaways that they had seen brought back in chains, branded with an R, or the ears cropped, remembering how they had seen them whipped and sent South with the chain gang.

Then another of the slaves, squatted by the fire, broke the silence. He used a long word: manumission. It was a word the master used. It was a promise that had been made to all of them. If they were faithful and hardworking, the master would set them free, manumit them, when he died.

Someone pointed out that such things did and could happen. There were free Negroes living in their own cabins on the edge of the woods, not far away from the plantation. Because these people were free, their children were born free. This was said with a covert glance at the tiny new baby, Minta or Minty, who lay close by Old Rit's side, in a corner of the cabin.

One of the sad dispirited slaves said that freedom lay only in death.

The bold ones said this was not true. They said you could run away, get to the North and be free. Slaves were disappearing all the time from the nearby farms and plantations. True, some of them were caught, brought back and sold South, but many of them were not. Quite often the masters and the overseers came back without the runaways.

They said they had sold them. But this was not necessarily true. Surely some of them, some of those young prime field hands, glossy-skinned, supple-jointed, surely some of those strong young men must have reached the North.

Yes, the others said, but how could one know? How be certain? Why did none of them ever come back? Why were they never seen again? It was cold in the North. Perhaps they died on the way, died of cold and hunger. Who could possibly know?

Then uncertainty and uneasiness filled the cabin again. More and more slaves were disappearing. Edward Brodas, the master, was selling them off. Each time the trader came to Maryland, came to Cambridge, the master sold another group of slaves. Nowadays it seemed as though he were raising slaves just to sell them. Breeding them, just like the farmers bred cows or sheep.

They were doing the same thing on the other plantations in Dorchester County—the Stewart plantation, and the Ross plantation—they were all selling slaves. Things were not going well with the masters. They needed money. The Georgia trader paid high prices, and if the masters were in debt, or a crop had failed, or they had been gambling heavily and losing, they sold off another lot of slaves.

When the slaves learned that they were to be sold, they ran away. They always knew when the decision had been reached to sell them. They were afraid of the living death that awaited them in the rice fields, on the great cotton plantations, the sugar plantations, in the deep South—and so ran away.

To the slaves those words, sold South, sold down the river, carried the sound of doom. The master used it as a threat to recalcitrant slaves. The runaways that were caught and brought back were immediately sold South, as a punishment for running away.

Thus the action on both sides was like a circle that went around and around, never ending. The master kept selling slaves because he needed money. The slaves, learning that they were about to be sold, would run away. The number of runaways from Maryland kept increasing. Especially from this Eastern Shore where the rivers and coves offered a direct route to the North, where the Choptank River curved and twisted in a northeasterly course, the whole length of the state—all the way to Delaware.

That night in the quarter, one of the bold young slaves said if one could get hold of a boat, and there were boats everywhere—rowboats, gunning skiffs, punts, because almost every plantation was near a cove or a creek or an inlet—one could get away.

This whispering about freedom, about runaways, about manumission, went on every night, in windowless slave cabins all over the South. Slaves everywhere knew what happened in Washington, Boston, New York, Norfolk, Baltimore, if it dealt with the subject of slavery. They knew it sometimes before the masters heard about it.

The close communication, the rapid exchange of information among the slaves, troubled and disturbed the masters. They said, half in joke, half seriously, that news seemed to travel down the wind, or else that it pulsed along from plantation to plantation, traveling over the tangle of grapevines and honeysuckle that grew in the woods.

On the plantation of Edward Brodas, the slaves knew when the Georgia trader arrived in Cambridge, the nearest city, and rented a room in the tavern. They knew it before Brodas knew it. The trader sent out printed notices of his arrival. Though most of the slaves could not read, there were a few who could, and they told the others what it said on the trader's handbills: "Will pay top prices for prime field hands. . . ."

On the night that Harriet (who would be known as Araminta, or Minty, or Minta) Ross was born, those words on the handbills were ever present in the minds of the slaves gathered in Old Rit's cabin. Before they said good night, they looked at the baby again. Someone said quietly, "Best thing to do is make sure she works in the Big House, sew or cook or weave—maybe be a nurse."

Old Rit drew the baby closer to her side, thinking, field hand, hot sun and long rows of cotton and the overseer's whip. Minty would *never* be a field hand if she had anything to do with it.

Then the slaves slipped out of the cabin as quietly as they had entered it, one at a time, bare feet making no sound at all on the hard smooth ground outside.

In that same year, 1820, the year of the Missouri Compromise, Thomas Garrett and his wife, Sarah, both Quakers, moved from Darby, Pennsylvania, to Wilmington, Delaware. Both of these people would, years later, know and admire Harriet Ross, though they would know her by a different name.

That year, John Brown, who was twenty years old, married the Widow Lusk, a short, plain-looking woman. He was in the tanning business in Hudson, Ohio, at the time of his marriage. Years later, he, too, would know and admire Harriet Ross.

2. The First Years

LIKE ALL the other babies in the quarter, Harriet Ross cut her first teeth on a piece of pork rind. The rind was tied to a string, and the string hung around her neck.

She learned to walk on the hard-packed earth outside the cabin, getting up, falling down, getting up again—a small naked creature, who answered to the name of Minta or Minty.

When she finally mastered the skill of walking, she began playing with other small children. All of the little ones, too young to run errands, were placed under the care of a woman, so old she could no longer work. She was a fierce-looking old woman, head wrapped in a white bandanna which she called a head rag. She sat crouched over, on the doorstep of her cabin, sucking on an empty clay pipe.

Though she was very old, she could still switch a small child with vigor, using a tough young shoot from a black gum tree, to enforce obedience. She never let the children out of her sight, warning them of the creek where they might drown, cautioning them about the nearby woods where they might get lost, shooing them out of the cabins lest they burn themselves in the hot ashes in the fire-

11

places. The children were afraid of her. She was toothless and she mumbled when she talked. The skin on her face was creased by a thousand wrinkles.

When she was in good humor, she told them stories about what she called the Middle Passage. The mumbling old voice evoked the clank of chains, the horror of thirst, the black smell of death, below deck in the hold of a slave ship. The children were too young to understand the meaning of the stories and yet they were frightened, standing motionless, listening to her, and shivering even if the sun was hot.

The mothers of these children worked in the fields. A few of them, like Old Rit, worked in or around the Big House.

Because the mothers were not at home, a family rarely ate together, all at the same time. The grownups ate from the skillet or black iron pot in which the food was cooked. Some of them ate from tin plates, balanced on the knees, eating for the most part with their hands.

The children were fed in a haphazard fashion, a bit of corn bread here, a scrap of pork there; occasionally they received a cup of milk, sometimes potatoes. When they were given corn-meal mush, it was poured into a large tray or trough. In winter the trough was placed on the floor of the cookhouse. In summer it was put outdoors, on the ground. The small children came running from all directions, with oyster shells, or pieces of shingle, to scoop up the mush. They swarmed around the trough of mush like so many small pigs.

Harriet, like the rest of the children, learned quickly that he who ate the fastest, got the most food. Yet they were always a little hungry, not starving, but with an emptiness inside them that was never quite assuaged.

She learned other things, too. On winter days, when the sun shone, she played on the south side of the cabin, where it was warmer. On cold rainy days, she huddled in a corner of the big chimney in the cookhouse, watching the constant stirring of the big iron pots. In the summer, when the sun was blistering hot, she stayed on the north side of the cabin because it was cooler there.

When Harriet was two years old, the whispering about freedom increased. In the quarter, at night, some of the slaves gathered together in the cabin that belonged to Ben, her father, and talked. It could hardly be called talking, it was conversation carried on under the breath, so that it was almost no sound at all.

On the way to Ben's cabin the slaves moved so quietly, so slowly, so stealthily, that they might have been part of the night itself. As they edged through the quarter, there was not even the soft sound of a bare foot on the hard-packed earth, not even the sound of breathing, not a cough, or a sneeze, nothing to indicate that a slave had left his own cabin and was paying a visit to another cabin.

There was fear and uneasiness all over the South that year. Fear on both sides. The masters were afraid of the slaves. The slaves were afraid of the masters.

Yet the slaves had to talk about this new and dreadful thing that had happened. Word of it seemed to have been carried by the wind, pushed along over the grapevines, from Charleston, South Carolina, to Wilmington, Delaware, and on down the Eastern Shore of Maryland, down to Alabama, Mississippi, Louisiana. It was discussed all through the South, in the slave cabins, in the big houses, whispered about, argued about, at night, just as it was in Ben's cabin.

They whispered about a man named Denmark Vesey. At first they had only bits of information about him, scraps of the story, and they slowly pieced it together, until they knew as much about him as the men who had tried and executed him.

Denmark Vesey was a free Negro. He bought his freedom when he was thirty-three. He had been a sailor. He could read and write. He was always reading the Bible. He told and retold the story of the children of Israel, and how they escaped from bondage, to a group of slaves who were his followers. He told them that all men were born equal. He said that it was degrading for a colored man to bow to a white man. Finally, he planned an insurrection, in which he and his followers were to kill all the white people in Charleston, South Carolina, and free the slaves. Before the insurrection was to take place, he quoted from the Book of Zechariah in the Old Testament: "Behold, the day of the Lord cometh, and thy spoil shall be divided in the midst of thee. For I will gather all nations against Jerusalem to battle; and the city shall be taken."

He had two men who worked closely with him, who helped him make the homemade pikes that were used in the insurrection. These men were Peter Poyas and Mingo Harth. They kept lists of the names of Denmark's followers, of the places where ammunition was kept, places where there were horses, and the names of slaves who looked after horses.

Two days before this uprising was to take place, the plot was revealed. One hundred thirty-one slaves, in and around Charleston, were arrested. Denmark and thirty-four others were hanged. None of them confessed. The story went that Peter Poyas said, "Die silent," when one of the slave conspirators appeared to be weakening under torture.

In the quarter, at night, when they talked of Denmark they said he had made life harder for the rest of them. They shivered even as they said it. It was no longer safe to walk along the roads at night, no longer safe to walk about the plantation where they lived, at night.

There were new laws now, because of Denmark. The new laws took away what little freedom of movement they had had. A slave caught on the road, alone, without a pass, would be whipped. Not by the overseer, or the master, but by any white man who happened to see him.

They were not supposed to talk to each other either. Two slaves standing talking would be whipped. They might be plotting servile insurrection, those long hard words that meant death to the master, death to the slave, too.

They had to be careful which songs they sang. They could no longer sing that fiery song, sound of thunder in the chorus:

> Go down, Moses,
> Way down in Egypt's land,
> Tell old Pharaoh,
> Let my people go!

Night after night they slipped into each other's cabins and talked of the man Denmark Vesey, of freedom, of the children of Israel and how they were led out of bondage. Inevitably, someone repeated the verse from Zechariah that Denmark had quoted: "Behold, the day of the Lord cometh . . . and the city shall be taken."

Then someone else voiced an objection. Things were infinitely worse because of Denmark and all his plots and plans for freedom. They could not hold church meetings of their own any more. It was now a crime to teach a slave to read or to write. The masters said that even a little learning made a slave discontented, unfit for a life of slavery.

Old Rit did not like all this talk of freedom and of Denmark Vesey. She said that the master had promised to free her and Ben and the children when he died. There was the sound of hope in her voice, mixed with fear. Because the master might forget to write it down in his will. Even if he did write it down, some of the crops might turn out bad, or he might have extra heavy debts to pay, or there might be a new overseer who would not like her or Ben—any of these things would mean that she and Ben would be sold, the children sold too, all of them scattered over the countryside.

Like the rest of the slaves, she feared change. She liked this place where they lived. The older children worked on nearby farms, so they were still together, as a family. True, the cabin was hot in summer, and filled with cold drafts in the winter, and the smoke from the fireplace half blinded them, but it was still a good place—it was their home.

The summers were warm, and there were creeks and inlets and streams in the nearby woods where they could catch fish, surreptitiously, of course, because they weren't supposed to. Sometimes they even fished in the Big Buckwater River, or set traps in the woods, and thus caught rabbits or squirrels and added a little variety to their food. After all, anyone would get tired of eating the same ashcake and fat back, or herring, day after day.

The master thought well of her and of Ben. Ben was big, broad-shouldered, a valuable hand. He worked in the woods, felling trees. She sometimes teased him about his ax. He was as fond of it as though it were a person. He said it was just right, it fitted his hands, almost worked by itself.

Ben was such a good workman, the master had placed him in charge of the slaves who cut the timber. Ben sometimes went all the way to the Bay (the Chesapeake) where the big logs were loaded on boats and sent to the shipbuilders in Baltimore.

Ever since the slaves started all this talk about Denmark Vesey, she had been uneasy, insecure. She worried about the children. They would never be really hers until they were free. Yet freedom was a dangerous thing to even think about. She wished the slaves would stop whispering about it all the time.

But every night, before these whispered conversations came to an end, one of the bolder slaves spoke of Denmark Vesey, voice pitched low, not much more than a murmuring in the firelit cabin. He talked about the slave who protested when Denmark had said that all men were equal. The slave had said, "But we are slaves." Denmark Vesey had said, "You deserve to be."

Old Rit hated the silence that always fell over the cabin afterward—a hush that spread and spread, and the shadows on the walls seemed to deepen. It made her heart beat faster, made her catch her breath.

In that same year, 1822, when Harriet was two years old, a twelve-year-old boy living in Lexington, Massachusetts, bought his first book, a Latin dictionary, with his own money. He earned the money by picking whortleberries (huckleberries) in his father's pasture, and selling them in Boston.

The boy's name was Theodore Parker. The Latin dictionary was the first of thirteen thousand volumes which he would eventually buy and, at his death, bequeath to the Boston Public Library.

Years later, Theodore Parker incurred the wrath of the pro-slavery forces in the country. He was called "the mad parson"; and he, too, eventually came to know Harriet Ross, but he knew her as Harriet Tubman.

3. Six Years Old

BY THE TIME Harriet Ross was six years old, she had unconsciously absorbed many kinds of knowledge, almost with the air she breathed. She could not, for example, have said how or at what moment she learned that she was a slave.

She knew that her brothers and sisters, her father and mother, and all the other people who lived in the quarter, men, women and children, were slaves.

She had been taught to say, "Yes, Missus," "No, Missus," to white women, "Yes, Mas'r," "No, Mas'r," to white men. Or, "Yes, sah," "No, sah."

At the same time, someone had taught her where to look for the North Star, the star that stayed constant, not rising in the east and setting in the west as the other stars appeared to do; and told her that anyone walking toward the North could use that star as a guide.

She knew about fear, too. Sometimes at night, or during the day, she heard the furious galloping of horses, not just one horse, several horses, thud of the hoofbeats along the road, jingle of harness. She saw the grown folks freeze into stillness, not moving, scarcely breathing, while they listened. She could not remember who first told her that those furious hoofbeats meant the patrollers were going

20

past, in pursuit of a runaway. Only the slaves said patterollers, whispering the word.

Old Rit would say a prayer that the hoofbeats would not stop. If they did, there would be the dreadful sound of screams. Because the runaway slave had been caught, would be whipped, and finally sold to the chain gang.

Thus Harriet already shared the uneasiness and the fear of the grownups. But she shared their pleasures, too. She knew moments of pride when the overseer consulted Ben, her father, about the weather. Ben could tell if it was going to rain, when the first frost would come, tell whether there was going to be a long stretch of clear sunny days. Everyone on the plantation admired this skill of Ben's. Even the master, Edward Brodas.

The other slaves were rather in awe of Ben because he could prophesy about the weather. Harriet stood close to him when he studied the sky, licked his forefinger and held it up to determine the direction of the wind, then announced that there would be rain or frost or fair weather.

There was something free and wild in Harriet because of Ben. He talked about the arrival of the wild ducks, the thickness of the winter coat of muskrats and of rabbits. He was always talking about the woods, the berries that grew there, the strange haunting cries of some of the birds, the loud sound their wings made when they were disturbed and flew up suddenly. He spoke of the way the owls flew, their feathers so soft that they seemed to glide, soundless, through the air.

Ben knew about rivers and creeks and swampy places. He said that the salt water from the Bay reached into the rivers and streams for long distances. You could stick your finger in the river water and lick it and you could taste the salt from the Bay.

He had been all the way to the Chesapeake. He had seen storms there. He said the Big Buckwater River, which lay off to the southeast of the plantation, was just a little stream compared to the Choptank, and the Choptank was less than nothing compared to the Bay.

All through the plantation, from the Big House to the stables, to the fields, he had a reputation for absolute honesty. He had never been known to tell a lie. He was a valued worker and a trusted one.

Ben could tell wonderful stories, too. So could her mother, Old Rit, though Rit's were mostly from the Bible. Rit told about Moses and the children of Israel, about how the sea parted so that the children walked across on dry land, about the plague of locusts, about how some of the children were afraid on the long journey to the Promised Land, and so cried out: "It had been better for us to serve the Egyptians, than that we should die in the wilderness."

Old Rit taught Harriet the words of that song that the slaves were forbidden to sing, because of the man named Denmark Vesey, who had urged the other slaves to revolt by telling them about Moses and the children of Israel. Sometimes, in

the quarter, Harriet heard snatches of it, sung under
the breath, almost whispered: "Go down,
Moses. . . ." But she learned the words so well
that she never forgot them.

She was aware of all these things and many
other things too. She learned to separate the days
of the week. Sunday was a special day. There was
no work in the fields. The slaves cooked in the
quarter and washed their clothes and sang and
told stories.

There was another special day, issue day, which
occurred at the end of the month. It was the day
that food and clothes were issued to the slaves.
One of the slaves was sent to the Big House, with
a wagon, to bring back the monthly allowance of
food. Each slave received eight pounds of pickled
pork or its equivalent in fish, one bushel of Indian
meal (corn meal), one pint of salt.

Once a year, on issue day, they received clothing. The men were given two tow-linen shirts,
two pairs of trousers, one of tow-linen, the other
woolen, and a woolen jacket for winter. The grownups received one pair of yarn stockings and a pair
of shoes.

The children under eight had neither shoes,
stockings, jacket nor trousers. They were issued
two tow-linen shirts a year—short, one-piece gar-
ments made of a coarse material like burlap,
reaching to the knees. These shirts were worn
night and day. They were changed once a week.
When they were worn out, the children went naked
until the next allowance day.

Men and women received a coarse blanket apiece. The children kept warm as best they could.

And so Harriet knew about Sunday which came once a week, about issue day which occurred once a month. She learned to divide time into larger segments too, based on changes of the season. There was seedtime when warmth began to creep back into the land. This was followed by the heat of summer. Then heat lay over the fields like a blanket; the bent backs of the field hands glistened in the sun, black backs wet with sweat. The fields seemed to shimmer in the sunlight.

The overseer, a white man on horseback, stayed on the edge of the field, in the shade. He seemed to shimmer too, as though all the heat of the sun were concentrated on him, a hot white light playing over him, even though he lingered in the shade. When for some reason the slaves stopped their rhythmical singing, he would shout, "Make a noise there! Make a noise there! Bear a hand!" and he cracked the black-snake whip he carried. It made a hissing sound like a snake.

After the heat of the summer, the year turned toward the fall, the nights began to grow cooler. Then came harvest, one of the best times of the year, when the big full moon lit the fields and the slaves worked late, singing songs that had a lilt in them, songs that were like a thanksgiving for the abundance of the crop.

Even better than that was the Christmas season. For Christmas was a long holiday, a whole stretch of days, until after New Year's. The slaves had little work to do. They kept the fires going, looked after the animals, milked the cows, fed and watered the livestock. The gaiety and laughter from the Big House reached all through the quarter. There were presents for everybody, and rare treats of sweet cakes and bits of candy, gay ribbons. The quarter was as filled with the sound of singing and of laughter as the Big House.

Harriet thought that Christmas was the very best time of all. By tradition there was no work. The holiday for the field slaves lasted as long as the Yule log burned in the fireplace at the Big House. So the people in the quarter spent days preparing the log. They chose a big one, so big that the strongest field hands bent their backs under its weight. They soaked it in water, so that it would burn slowly and for a long time.

It was cold at Christmastime, cold in the winter there on the Eastern Shore. Yet Harriet liked the winter. She watched the flickering light from the fire. It cast long dancing shadows against the smoke-darkened walls. She knew and liked the damp earthy smell of the dirt floor, even though they slept on the floor, huddled under thin ragged blankets, aware of the chill. Even though on windy nights, puffs of smoke blew back down the chimney, making them cough, yet she still liked the cold months when the fire was lit.

At night, inside the cabin, she felt safe. But with the coming of morning, she was always a little frightened. In the early morning dark, not yet sunrise, but a grayness in the sky, a slight lifting of the darkness, she heard and recognized the long low notes of the overseer's horn, calling the field hands to work. Then she would hear the sound of running feet, sound of curses, the thud, thud of blows, falling on the head and back of the last field hand out of the quarter.

And so at six, Harriet already knew fear and uneasiness. She knew certain joys too, the joy of singing, the warmth from a pine-knot fire in a fireplace, the flickering light that served as decoration, making shadows on the walls, changing, moving, dancing, concealing the lack of furniture.

She was accustomed to the scratchy feel of the tow-linen shirt she wore. Because she went barefooted, the soles of her feet were calloused, but the toes were straight, never having known the pinch of new shoes or any kind of foot covering.

She was a solemn-eyed, shy little girl, slow of speech, but quick to laugh. She was always singing or humming, under her breath, pausing in her play to look upward, watching the sudden free flight of the birds, listening to the cherokee of the redwing blackbirds, watching a squirrel run up the trunk of a tree, in the nearby woods, studying the slow drift of cumulus clouds across a summer sky.

This period of carefree idleness was due to end soon. The fierce old woman who looked after the children kept telling Minta that things would change.

Whenever she saw the little girl stop to look at the trees, the sky, she repeated the same harsh-voiced warning: "Overseer'll be settin' you a task

any day now. Then you won't be standin' around
with your mouth hangin' open, lookin' at nothin'
all day long. Overseer'll keep you movin'."

*Thomas Jefferson, author of the Declaration of
Independence, died at Monticello in Virginia on
July 4, 1826. He was eighty-three years old.*

*His original draft of the Declaration contained
a "vehement philippic against Negro slavery." Congress eliminated this. But these words were left intact: "We hold these truths to be self-evident, that
all men are created equal, that they are endowed
by their Creator with certain unalienable rights, that
among these are Life, Liberty and the pursuit of
Happiness."*

*This idea, part of Jefferson's legacy to America,
written down in one of the country's noblest documents, was incompatible with the idea of legalized
slavery. Yet it was an integral part of the heritage
of all Americans, and so it troubled the minds of
men in the North and in the South, long after Jefferson's death.*

*Many a slave carried the dream of freedom in his
heart because of these words of Jefferson's. Not because the slave had read them, but because they
were written down somewhere, and other people
had read them, and ideas are contagious—particularly ideas that concern the rights of man.*

4. Hired Out

IN THE SUMMER of 1826, Harriet was six years old and, by plantation standards, big enough to work. She carried water to the field hands, and listened to their rhythmical singing, watched how the movement of their hands, their bodies, was paced to the rhythm of the song.

She was old enough to have a sense of family. She enjoyed being with her father and her mother, her brothers and sisters. There were ten children now, either living in the cabin, because they worked on the master's plantation, or else living so near it that they could visit Ben and Old Rit.

That year, in the fall, a woman drove up to the Big House in a wagon. She went inside and stayed for quite a while. Almost as soon as she arrived, word of what she wanted was relayed through the quarter.

This woman had come to see the master. She wanted to hire one of the master's slaves, preferably a girl, and young, because she couldn't pay very much. The woman said that any of the little ones running around the cabins would do. The house slave who brought this whispered news to the quarter said that the woman wasn't quality. She was barely a cut above poor white folks, when compared to the master. She was a weaver, and the wife of a man named James Cook, a man who hunted and trapped for a living.

Before six-year-old Harriet knew what was happening, she was seated in the wagon, beside this strange white woman who was now her mistress. She had been "hired out" by the master, Edward Brodas. Mrs. James Cook was going to pay him a small sum a month for the services of Harriet.

Harriet sat in the wagon, frightened, listening to the clop-clop of the horses' feet. They kept going farther and farther away from the quarter on the plantation, where she had been born and brought up. They went through the woods, along an old road, called a rolling road, though she did not know it. These roads were made in the days when tobacco was the chief crop on the Eastern Shore, and hogsheads of tobacco were rolled down to the wharves, and the boat landings, and the roads thus made still bear the name "rolling road."

When the wagon finally stopped near a house, Harriet was disappointed in it. It was not like the Big House. It was built of logs, just like the cabins in the quarter. But at least it was near a river, though she never knew the name of the river. Once she got inside, she found it had more than one room, and it had an upstairs. She had never before been inside a house where people had a separate room in which they slept. For she had never been in the Big House. There was no reason why she should. Even Old Rit didn't go there—unless she was sent for.

Mrs. Cook was a weaver. She spent most of the day in front of a big loom, head bent, arms moving back and forth. Harriet was supposed to help her. She stood for hours, winding yarn, her hands clumsy, unaccustomed to the job she had to do, the thread catching, catching on the rough places on her fingers. The air was filled with fuzz and lint, so that she kept sneezing and dropping the yarn.

It seemed to Harriet that the clatter of the loom and the whirr and thump of the spinning wheel went on day and night, too. It confused her. She longed to be back in the quarter, in the cabin with Ben and Rit. She was afraid. She was lonesome.

She hated the inside of the house. She slept in the kitchen, in a corner near the fireplace; toward morning, when the fire went out, she slept with her feet tucked in and under the warm ashes because it was so cold at night. These people fed her scraps of food, much as they might have fed a dog.

The woman said Harriet was clumsy, slow, no help at all, so the man set her to watching his trap lines. He had his traps set for muskrats.

It was cold by the river but Harriet didn't mind. It was quiet there. She was away from the clatter of the loom. She could breathe without getting her mouth and nose full of lint. As she walked the length of Cook's trap line she saw an occasional gunning skiff, heard the wild free crying of the water birds, watched them fly up, wings spread wide.

She learned to stand still, on the bank of the river, and thus she saw the muskrats swimming, noses above water, watched them dive. She discovered the burrows they made in the bank, built with mud and bits of straw. By careful watching, she was able to distinguish the dark brown fur of a muskrat, near the burrow, though they were the same color as the mud along the bank.

One morning she woke up coughing, eyes watering, feeling sick, hot, utterly miserable. Mrs. Cook said that slaves were always pretending to be sick in order to avoid work, that young as Minty was, she too had learned to slack off on her work; they seemed to be born knowing how to do this.

So James Cook sent Minty out to inspect his trap lines. She stumbled along, head down, vision blurred by the watering of her eyes. She wasn't crying—but her eyes kept filling up with tears. The water in the river was so cold that she shuddered as she waded along the edge. She had to wade to see if the traps had been sprung. She bent over, shivering, examining a trap, not liking the scaly look of the tails of the muskrats and yet not liking to see them caught in the traps. They wouldn't swim any more, wouldn't dive any more, after they were caught. They had an unpleasant musky smell but she still didn't like to see them held fast in the traps.

When she went back to the house, a small bent-over figure, shivering and shaking, it was obvious that she was really sick. Mrs. Cook got a blanket and threw it over her, wondering audibly what was wrong with Minty.

She was so sick that Old Rit heard about it, and went to Edward Brodas and asked him to take

Minty away from Cook's, to let her come home where Rit could look after her. The master consented. He was fond of Old Rit and he did not want to lose Harriet if he could help it. Sometimes there in the quarter, when they nursed themselves, they got well; they all seemed to have an inexplicable knowledge of the curative power of the roots and herbs that grew in the woods and the meadows.

Rit nursed Harriet back to health. It was six weeks before she was really well. She had the measles. Because of the wading in the cold water of the river, she developed bronchitis. Rit kept giving her a hot and bitter brew, made from the root of a plant that Ben brought back from the woods.

There was always a huskiness in Harriet's voice after that. It stayed there for the rest of her life, an undertone that made her singing voice memorable. It lent an added timbre to her speaking voice.

As soon as Harriet recovered, was once more playing with the young children, running and laughing, singing, listening to the stories told by the old folks, the master sent her back to the house of James Cook.

Rit grumbled about it, first to herself, and then to Ben when he came home from the woods.

"Minty's back at Cook's," she said.

He nodded, neither approving nor disapproving.

She thought, he already knows it, probably word got to him in the woods. "They're poor folks," she said. "Not much better than white trash. Can't afford to own any slaves. Can't even afford to hire full-grown ones. So they take Minty."

He said calmly, "Well, at least—"

Rit went on, her voice raised. "They get her for almost nothing. About all she costs 'em is for her food and there ain't much of that from the look of her when she came back to the quarter. Nothing but skin drawn over bones. No meat on her at all."

Ben said, "Maybe she'll learn to be a weaver."

"Maybe she won't," Rit answered sharply as though he were arguing with her. "That's another thing. Quality don't work at nothing like that. The wives don't work and they don't give the orders. Shows what kind of folks the Cooks are. She gives the orders. She works at the weaving. Weaves other folks' cloth for them—"

Then she stopped talking, and sighed, thinking, of course if Minty did learn to weave, it would be good. She'd never know the bite of the overseer's whip, never know what it felt like to hold a hoe in rough, work-hardened hands, never give off the choking stink of the field hand.

She said, hopefully, "Maybe she'll learn to be a weaver."

Ben nodded. "Perhaps," he said cautiously. "If not a weaver—something else. She's smarter'n all the rest put together."

When Minta, or Minty, whose Christian name was Harriet, went back to the Cooks, she soon learned that she was to stay indoors and learn to weave. She was not to walk Cook's trap lines any more.

She felt like the muskrats, one moment she had

seen them diving and swimming in the river, and then suddenly click! and they were caught fast in the trap. She remembered that some of them had fought to free themselves, tearing fur and flesh to get free.

She decided that she simply would not learn to weave. She would not! She hated being inside the house with the loom and the spinning wheel and the endless hanks of yarn. These was always lint in the air. She was always cold. She did not get enough to eat. She wanted to go home where she could be outdoors.

The woman that she called her mistress was always cross. She kept telling her that she was stupid, stupid, stupid.

And so, finally, Cook's wife sent Harriet back to the Brodas plantation. She said that she was unteachable, intractable, hopelessly stupid.

Early in the nineteenth century, the dream of freedom had begun spreading through the slave cabins on all the plantations. Almost every night, somewhere in the South, a slave slipped away from the quarter. They hid in swamps. They walked incredible distances. Some of them reached the North and freedom. Others were caught and brought back in chains. There were few plantations that could boast that they had never had a slave run away.

By 1826 there were so many fugitive slaves living in Canada that plantation owners in Maryland and Kentucky persuaded Henry Clay, then Secretary of State, to ask the Canadian Government to work out a plan whereby these fugitives, worth thousands of dollars, could be lawfully returned to their owners.

The Americans waited eagerly for an answer. It was a long time coming, and when it finally arrived, it was most unsatisfactory. The Canadian Government stated that the request of the American Secretary of State had been received. And that was all. There was no suggestion made as to how American slaveowners could obtain the slaves who had taken refuge in Canada.

5. Flight

EVERY NIGHT in the quarter, after the children were asleep, Old Rit and Ben talked about Harriet. Old Rit started the conversation.

"What's going to happen to Minty?" she asked.

Ben stirred under the ragged quilt, and then turned over. "You have to trust in the Lord, Rit. He'll take care of her."

Rit ignored his reply. "Here she is back on the plantation again. She's seven years old and she hasn't learned anything special. You know the Master isn't going to keep her around here, just kicking up her heels and eating her head off. What'll happen to her?"

This time Ben did not answer. They both knew things weren't going well with the master. He needed money. He was hiring out more and more of his slaves. He was selling more and more of them each year. The plantation was beginning to have a ragged, uncared for look. The fences were down. Honeysuckle and bull briar were slowly taking over the big fields. The outbuildings needed repair.

Rit touched Ben on the arm, lightly, to attract his attention. Then she whispered, "The trader's back in Cambridge again. He's got the big front room at the tavern. Less than two months and he's back again. He didn't used to come so often."

She waited for Ben to say something, to reassure her. He knew just as she did that when the trader got ready to leave, some of the master's prime hands were sure to go with him. Well, not exactly with him. They'd go with the chain gang, walking down that long, terrible road that ended in New Orleans or Natchez, chained two by two, and another chain down through the middle of the group, and each slave chained to that, too. She'd heard the white folks call it a coffle or drove, but to her it was always simply the chain gang.

"Nothing's going to happen to Minty," Old Ben said, sharply. "I'll see that it don't."

The sharpness in his voice told her that he was thinking about the chain gang too, and remembering their two little ones, just about the size of Minty, who had gone away like that. One minute they had been carrying water to the field hands, and the next minute they were in a lot with the other slaves that had been sold, sort of thrown in for good measure, and then—gone—gone with the chain gang.

But there's nothing Ben can do, she thought. He can try, of course. But the trader had a reputation for driving a hard bargain, and if the master needed the money, and one extra child meant a slightly better price for the lot—why, even Ben wouldn't be able to stop the sale.

Rit gave a long sigh. "I wish the old days were back again. The days when the Master was rich and just raised tobacco, just nothing but tobacco. And everybody worked. Even the little slaves helped squash those fat juicy hornworms that get on the backside of the tobacco leaves. And everybody had plenty to eat and we all felt safe. In the old days the Master never sold off any of his slaves. Everybody knew that and—"

Ben agreed with her. "Yes," he said slowly, "things was better then. It seems like they seesaw more now. He grows a little corn. Then maybe there's too much rain, or maybe not enough rain, so the crop's no good. Now he's selling the big timber off to the shipbuilders. Pretty soon there won't be any more of them big stands of oaks. We keep hacking 'em down, day after day we're hacking 'em down. What's he going to do when his timber's gone?"

"You know what he's going to do," Rit said impatiently. "He's going to keep on raising slaves and selling them off. He gets enough money just from that. He don't have to bother to have his land worked any more. He's just living off his slaves."

Living off his slaves, she thought, and little Minty doesn't know how to cook or sew, and the slave trader is in Cambridge—and maybe tomorrow he'll be riding out here.

"Oh, Ben," she said, "what's going to happen to Minty?"

"I guess maybe we just better pray to the good Lord to look out for her," he said. "We just better pray—"

A few days later, Harriet was hired out again, as a child's nurse. Rit said, "May the Lord be praised, it's an answer to my prayer, to my prayer. May the Lord be praised."

Once again, Harriet, the small girl in the tow-linen shirt, barefooted, feet not touching the floor of the wagon, sat listening to the clop-clop of horses' hoofs, listening to the creak of a wagon that was carrying her farther and farther away from home.

Her forehead was wrinkled by a frown because she kept thinking: Where am I going this time? How long will it take to get there? Why do I have to go anywhere?

Suppose she didn't like the people. What could she do about it? She wouldn't know how to get back home.

Finally the wagon stopped in front of a big house. She never did know where it was located, near what town, how far away from the Brodas plantation. But she soon knew what she was supposed to do. She looked after Miss Susan's baby and helped with the housework, too. It wasn't a big family, just Miss Susan and her husband, and the baby, and Miss Emily, a sister of Miss Susan's who was visiting.

That first morning, Miss Susan told her to go and sweep the parlor and dust it. Harriet was awed by the room. There was a thick carpet on the floor, soft and springy under her feet, like walking on layers of pine needles, and there were so many different kinds of chairs and tables, and the wood around the fireplace was carved into a pattern. She'd never seen anything like it.

She swept as hard as she could, and then immediately dusted all the dark shiny wood of the furniture.

Miss Susan said, "Have you finished?" and came in to run her fingers over the shiny surface of the chairs and tables. Her fingers were coated with dust. "Do it again," she snapped. "Are you just plain stupid? Why, you haven't dusted in here at all. You do it right—or—"

Harriet swept again, and then dusted, getting more and more frightened. Miss Susan said it wasn't done properly and went and got a whip and kept whipping her and shouting at her; and Harriet screamed.

She heard a voice calling, "Susan! Susan! What are you doing? What is the matter?"

Miss Emily had heard the screams and came downstairs, protesting, "Why do you whip the child, Susan, for not doing what she has never been taught to do? Leave her to me a few minutes, and you will see that she will soon learn how to sweep and dust a room."

Harriet learned how to clean the house. She looked after the baby, too. In later life, she said, "I was so little that I had to sit on the floor and have the baby put in my lap. That baby was always in my lap except when it was asleep or its mother was feeding it."

Miss Susan said that the baby mustn't be allowed to cry. Harriet had to keep rocking it so it wouldn't cry. Every night the same thing happened. She sat on the floor and rocked the cradle back and forth, back and forth, until the baby went to sleep. Then her head drooped, her eyelids closed, her hand started slipping, slipping, slipping away from the dark polished wood of the cradle. Finally she slept, on the floor, by the cradle.

Then the baby would wail, suddenly, a thin, high, piercing sound. Miss Susan would wake up, furious, and reach for the whip she kept on a little shelf behind her bed.

Harriet finally reached a point in exhaustion where she was past needing sleep, where she snatched it in brief moments, head nodding, eyes closed, and yet not really asleep, prepared to start rocking the cradle before the baby woke up and cried.

Even so, sometimes she went sound asleep, to be awakened by the wailing of the baby. She was whipped so often that the back of her neck was covered with scars, crisscrossed with scars, so deep that they would be visible for the rest of her life. Finally she learned to sleep without really going to sleep, learned to listen while still asleep, head nodding, eyes closed, but all her senses alerted to the slightest movement from the cradle, listening, listening, and yet asleep. So that if the baby stirred, she started rocking the cradle.

She thought of running away, and didn't. She did not know how to reach the Brodas plantation, did not know in which direction to walk, assuming that she could have got away from the house. She had no idea how far it was. It had seemed an interminable journey when the overseer brought her to Miss Susan's in a wagon.

Sometimes Miss Susan and her husband went out to parties. Then there were plumes on Miss Susan's bonnet, and she wore a silk dress, soft, swishy, and embroidered petticoats underneath, making a rustling sound when she walked. She smelled of orrisroot. And the master would smile at Miss Susan, and toy with his watch chain.

On those nights, the baby cried and cried, while Harriet slept. Harriet slept and yet she was listening. Not for the baby. Ears straining, even in sleep, for the sound of footsteps on the stairs, not even footsteps, just the creak of the stairs, and she was awake, because it meant Miss Susan was coming home. Thus she learned to stay alert even though she was deeply, restfully asleep.

During the day, she toyed with the idea of running away. Then she would thrust the thought from her as impossible.

Yet she did run away. Years afterward, she described what happened in these words: "One morning, after breakfast, Miss Susan had the baby, and I stood by the table waiting until I was to take it; near me was a bowl of lumps of white sugar. My mistress got into a great quarrel with her husband; she had an awful temper, and she would scold and storm and call him all kinds of names.

"Now you know, I never had anything good, no sweet, no sugar; and that sugar, right by me, did look so nice, and mistress's back was turned to me

42

while she was fighting with her husband, so I just put my fingers in the sugar bowl to take one lump and maybe she heard me for she turned and saw me.

"The next minute she had the rawhide down. I give one jump out of the door and I saw that *they* came after me, but I just flew and *they* didn't catch me. I ran and I ran and I passed many a house, but I didn't dare to stop for they all knew my mistress and they would send me back."

She ran until she was exhausted. She kept looking over her shoulder. After a while she didn't see Miss Susan and her husband. She decided that they must have got tired and stopped chasing her. She slowed her pace, then at the thought of having to go back to Miss Susan and whatever form of punishment she and her husband would have devised, she started running again.

She said, "By and by when I was almost tuckered out, I came to a great big pigpen. There was an old sow there, and perhaps eight or ten little pigs. I was too little to climb into it, but I tumbled over the high part and fell in on the ground; I was so beaten out that I could not stir.

"And there I stayed from Friday until the next Tuesday, fighting with those little pigs for the potato peelings and the other scraps that came down in the trough. The old sow would push me away when I tried to get her children's food, and I was awfully afraid of her. By Tuesday I was so starved I knew I had to go back to my mistress.

I didn't have anywhere else to go, even though I knew what was coming. So I went back."

That same year, 1827, Henry Clay, who was still Secretary of State, appealed to the Canadian Government again. He asked for some kind of agreement in regard to the return of the hundreds of fugitive slaves living in Canada. After five months had gone by, the Canadians said: "It is utterly impossible to agree to a stipulation for the surrender of fugitive slaves."

In the city of New York, two Negroes, John Russwurm and the Reverend Mr. Samuel Cornish, began to publish Freedom's Journal, *the first Negro newspaper in the United States.*

6. The Underground Road

HARRIET WAS BACK on the Brodas plantation, back in the slave quarter. Miss Susan brought her back and told the master that Minta wasn't "worth a sixpence."

Old Rit sniffed her contempt for Miss Susan when she saw Minta. The child was little better than skin and bones. She was as filthy as though she'd been living in a hog wallow, and her neck and back were covered with scars, old scars crisscrossed with fresh ones from the beating Miss Susan and her husband had given her because she ran away.

It was slow work, but Old Rit got the fresh scars healed up, and then when Harriet began to get a little flesh on her bones, Brodas hired her out again.

In a way, Harriet had won a victory—though Rit did not think so. Harriet worked in the fields from then on. Brodas hired her out to a man who kept her out of doors. She loaded wood on wagons, split rails, and knew more about mules and hoes and plows than she did about the interior of a house. Despite her strong sturdy body, she was still a child. Yet she was often ordered to perform jobs that would have taxed the strength of a full-grown, able-bodied man. If she failed in any of these backbreaking jobs, she was beaten.

Her appearance began to change. The solemn-eyed, shy little girl, hesitant of speech, had disappeared. She was replaced by a sullen-eyed creature, the lids hanging heavily over the eyes. She had the calloused work-hardened hands of a field slave.

She no longer wore the tow-linen shirt, the one garment worn by the children. She wore a long one-piece dress, tied around the middle with a piece of rope. She looped the skirts up when she was in the field. She was still barefooted.

She worked from dawn to dusk, worked in the rain, in the heat of the sun. Her muscles hardened. She sang when she was in the fields or working in the nearby woods. Her voice was unusual because of the faint huskiness. Once having heard it, people remembered it. The low notes were rich and deep. The high notes were sweet and true. Like the other slaves, she made up the words and the melody of most of the songs that she sang, never singing them exactly the same way.

In 1831, Harriet started wearing a bandanna. It was made from a piece of brilliantly colored cotton cloth. She wound it around her head, deftly, smoothly, and then tied it in place, pulling the knots tight and hard. This new headgear was an indication that she was no longer regarded as a child. These colorful bandannas were worn by young women; they were a symbol of maturity.

Though the life she led was cruelly hard, she was more nearly content than she had ever been before. She was working outdoors. She felt free in the fields. No matter how hard the job assigned to her, she could always pause for a moment in her work and watch the slow drift of the clouds overhead, study the swift flight of the birds. Even in summer, when heat waves rose from the land, there was a fresh smell from the woods close by.

Sometimes this short, straight-backed young girl hummed under her breath, or sang, while she hoed the corn or tugged on the reins when a refractory mule refused to budge. True, work in the fields had calloused her hands, but it had given her a strong, erect body. She carried her head proudly as she sang.

That year, 1831, when Harriet regarded herself as sufficiently grown up to wear a bandanna, she kept hearing a strange, fascinating story, told and retold, in the quarter, in the fields. This same story about a slave named Tice Davids was being told in the Big House, too. But with a difference. The slaves told it with relish, the masters with distaste.

Tice Davids ran away from his master in Kentucky. He planned to cross the Ohio River at Ripley. But his master followed so close behind him that Tice had to jump in the river and swim across.

The master hunted for a boat, and while hunting, never lost sight of Tice, kept watching his head, just above the water, as he swam toward the opposite shore. Once in the boat, the master followed him, saw him plainly, swimming faster and faster. The master drew so near to him that when Tice stood up in the water and started to run, he could see the water splashing about his thighs. He saw him reach the shore. The master grounded the boat, jumped out—not more than five minutes behind the slave.

He never saw Tice Davids again. He combed the countryside; he searched the antislavery town of Ripley. He knew that the town had a reputation of being hostile to slaveholders, had heard vaguely of a Reverend John Rankin who served as watchdog and guardian of runaways—Even so. Tice Davids had disappeared right before his master's eyes.

The master went back to Kentucky and told about this strange disappearance, how his slave, Tice, had literally vanished before his eyes. Puzzled, disturbed more than he cared to admit, he explained this mystery by saying, "He must have gone on an underground road."

Harriet was puzzled by this story. She kept thinking about it. Was there a road that ran under the ground? Was that how Tice Davids had escaped from his master? If Tice could find it, could other people find it, too?

People in the border states, who had been sheltering runaway slaves, helped further the mystery of an underground road. The new steam trains were being talked about everywhere. A rumor started, and spread, to the effect that there was an underground railroad too.

The free Negroes, the Quakers, the Methodists, the German farmers, who helped runaway slaves in Ohio, Pennsylvania, New York, started using phrases and words suited to the idea of a railroad.

They called themselves conductors, stationmasters, brakemen. Their houses and barns and haystacks, and the unsuspected secret passages inside the big farmhouses, were called depots and stations. They referred to the runaways as passengers, parcels, boxes, bales of black wool. Large parcels were grownups; small parcels were children.

In 1831 there were many people like the young Harriet, who believed that there really was a steam train that ran through a deep underground tunnel from South to North, and that a slave who could board it in the South, at some unknown point, would emerge a free man, in a free state, when the train came up out of the ground, snorting and puffing, leaving a trail of smoke and cinders behind it. Certainly the story of Tice Davids suggested that this was true.

This mysterious underground railroad was spoken of, in whispers, in the quarter on the Brodas plantation, just as it was on all the other plantations.

In that same year, in August, in October, in November, the slaves in the quarter and the masters in the Big Houses began to talk about another story. In the quarter, the name of the man who was involved was never spoken aloud. It was always whispered, as though the land, the trees, the sky, the rivers and coves had ears. For this was a horror story. Its details were known all over the United States. Like the other slaves, Harriet knew the story as accurately and as completely as though she had been an eyewitness to the event.

It was the story of Nat Turner. He was a slave,

in Southampton, Virginia. He was called The Prophet. He was a preacher.

When he was a boy, growing up, his mother told him, over and over, that he would be like Moses. He would lead his people out of slavery as Moses had led the children of Israel out of bondage in Egypt. She taught him verses and whole chapters of the Bible which she had memorized. He memorized them too, especially the ones that dealt with the prophets in the Old Testament.

He was a silent, brooding man, given to fasts and contemplation, going often, alone, into the caves of the mountains, in the section of Virginia where he lived. He believed himself to be a prophet. He claimed that he saw visions.

On the night of August 20, 1831, he said to six of his followers: "Our race is to be delivered from bondage, and God has appointed us as the men to do His bidding; I am told to slay all the whites we encounter, men, women and children . . . it is necessary that in the commencement of this revolution all the whites we meet must die."

They set out together, Nat Turner and his six followers, and at every plantation where they stopped, other slaves joined them, until there were seventy of them altogether. They killed sixty white persons, men, women and children, found on plantations within a radius of twenty miles.

The local militia and Federal troops were called in to quell this unplanned and unrehearsed insurrection. All through the South, slaveholders were terrified. Though one hundred Negroes were killed in the process of putting down this revolt, Nat Turner could not be found. He stayed hidden in a cave in Southampton County for two months. He was finally found, and executed on November 11, 1831.

On the Brodas plantation, the slaves whispered about The Prophet too.

Harriet, wearing her first bandanna, working in the fields, thought about him, brooded about him. There was no question but that they all wanted freedom—but at such a price—

After November 11th, the whispering in the cabins went on endlessly, night after night, while the fire died down in the fireplaces. Every night in the quarter on the Brodas plantation, Harriet heard an old black woman hunched over, clay pipe in her mouth, mutter, "Eye for eye, tooth for tooth, hand for hand, foot for foot, burning for burning, wound for wound, stripe for stripe." The fire flared and set the shadows on the walls to trembling.

After the Nat Turner insurrection, fear hung over the plantations from Virginia on down through Maryland, down to Louisiana, Alabama, Mississippi. The slaveholders lived in dread because the most faithful house slave might at any moment become another Nat, attacking the master, in the dead of night, with no warning.

New laws were passed in the slave states and the old laws were more rigidly enforced. Nat Turner had been a silent, brooding slave. Get rid of the silent ones. He had been a preacher, he had talked about the children of Israel, about Moses—therefore there must be no more Sunday schools for children who were slaves, no more separate church services for the slaves. They must not be permitted to congregate anywhere, at any time. Must not be allowed to talk freely to each other. Under no circumstances must they be permitted to learn to read and write. Make it a crime for anyone to teach them.

Once again the slaves were forbidden to sing "Go down, Moses," the song with the sound of thunder in the chorus: "Let my people go!"

Harriet thought that the ghost of Nat Turner had joined the ghost of Denmark Vesey, the carpenter and free man. Twin ghosts now haunted the Big Houses, the fields, the masters, the overseers, the slave traders, the slave drivers. She wondered if they hovered over the coffle of slaves being driven down one of the old overland routes to Natchez or New Orleans, whispering taunts, crying revenge, bloody revenge, revolt, bloody revolt.

The Virginia Assembly met in December, 1831. The subject of slavery was introduced because some of the counties, alarmed by the Nat Turner insurrection, had petitioned for the gradual emancipation of the slaves or for abolition of slavery.

Two farmers, whose landholdings were small when compared to the great areas controlled by some of the Virginia slaveholders, were outspoken in their criticism of the institution of slavery.

Phillip Bolling: "We talk of freedom while slavery exists in the land, and speak with horror of the tyranny of the Turk; but we foster an evil which the best interests of the community require shall be removed and to which we trace the cause of the depression of eastern Virginia."

Henry Berry: "Pass as severe laws as you will to keep these unfortunate creatures in ignorance, it is in vain unless you can extinguish that spark of intellect which God has given them. . . . can man be in the midst of freedom and not know what freedom is? A death struggle must come in which one or the other class is extinguished forever."

7. "Shuck This Corn"

IT WAS THE FALL of the year. The corn and wheat were being harvested. The harvesting of the corn was, traditionally, the occasion for rejoicing. The days were getting shorter, the nights were perceptibly cooler, the year was turning toward the Christmas season and the long holiday which the entire countryside would celebrate—both the masters and the slaves.

In Dorchester County there were parties on the big plantations, the clink of glasses, the sound of singing, carriages arriving at the Big House.

In the fields, late in the day, afternoon merging into night, a cornhusking bee was in progress on the Brodas plantation. The corn had been stacked in a great mound. The master had invited his friends to send their slaves to help shuck the corn.

The slaves had mounded the corn up, higher, higher, higher, dark hands lifting the ears of corn, slight rustle from the ears, two or three hundred slaves moving around the great stack.

When the corn was mounded up, the best singer among the slaves, the one with the highest, clearest, truest voice, climbed to the top of the stack and led off the singing. The song was always improvised, except for the repeated Oh! Oh! Oh! of the chorus.

There was something wild and beautiful about this singing; the sun was going down, the feel of frost in the air, and the knowledge that once the song was done, they would husk the corn, swiftly, singing something else, hands moving in time to the beat of whatever the new song would be, a song in praise of the land, the harvest, a kind of propitiation to the land, and a song of thanksgiving, too:

I

> *Master's slaves are slick and fat,*
> > *Oh! Oh! Oh!*
> *Shine just like a beaver hat,*
> > *Oh! Oh! Oh!*

Refrain:
> *Turn out here and shuck this corn,*
> > *Oh! Oh! Oh!*
> *Biggest pile seen since I was born,*
> > *Oh! Oh! Oh!*

II

> *Barrett's slaves are lean and thin*
> > *Oh! Oh! Oh!*
> *Can put their food on the end of a pin*
> > *Oh! Oh! Oh!*

Refrain:
> *Turn out here and shuck this corn,*
> > *Oh! Oh! Oh!*

Biggest pile seen since I was born,
Oh! Oh! Oh!

One of Barrett's slaves stood silent at the foot of the big pile of corn. Harriet watched him, aware that the overseer was watching him, too. A silent slave was not liked by overseers, because a silent slave was probably brooding about escape or revolt. He might have persuaded the others to take part in whatever it was that he was plotting. He might be another Denmark Vesey or Nat Turner— She watched him and felt a prickle of fear run through her.

As that last high-pitched rhythmic Oh! Oh! Oh! rang out across the field, the slaves set to work husking the corn, racing with each other, to see who could husk the most in the shortest possible time. They started singing a new song, its tempo faster and faster, the movement of their hands paced to the rhythm of the song, and the sound of the rustling of the husks of the corn like an accompaniment.

Harriet watched Barrett's slave, her own hands moving swiftly, stripping the husks from the corn, enjoying the fading light, the coolness that lay over the land, the look of the cornfield now that the crop was harvested, noticing all these things, and working, and yet watching the big young man who stood silent, whose hands moved slowly, desultorily.

She leaned over to pick up an ear of corn, and when she looked for him, he was moving away. His swiftly moving figure was in strange contrast to the languorous slow motion of his hands just a few minutes before.

The overseer did not see him until he was half-way across the field. He called to him, ordering him to come back. The big young man kept going, faster now. The overseer followed him, the black-snake whip in his hand.

Harriet went too. There would be trouble. She knew there was going to be trouble, she could always tell when it was coming, by the peculiar fluttering of her heart. It was a warning signal, and it was telling her now that something dreadful was going to happen.

They went down one of the old rolling roads, the slave running, and the overseer running too. He was not on horseback, he had not expected trouble, in the middle of a husking bee, an occasion for frolicking and fun. Harriet followed close behind.

The slave ducked inside the door of the store at the crossroads. The overseer went after him. Harriet heard him say that he would whip him right then and there, and thus teach him not to run away from his work. He called for help, to tie the slave. He ordered Harriet to help hold him.

She did not move. She stood there just inside the door watching these two. The overseer could not hope to whip the slave unless someone helped tie him up. The big young man who belonged to Barrett dodged past the overseer, head down, and was through the door and gone—just that fast.

Harriet moved in front of the doorway, stood there, blocking it. The overseer, startled by this sudden obstructing body, planted squarely in the doorway, turned away from the door, picked up a two-pound weight from the counter, and hurled it at the fleeing slave.

The weight missed the slave. It struck Harriet in the forehead, leaving a great open gash there. She was thrown backward from the force of the blow. She was brought back to the quarter, unconscious, bleeding.

In the quarter the slaves came to look at her. They said that she would surely die. No one could survive with a great hole in the head like that, with the good warm blood, the life's blood draining out. So much blood. Even Brodas came to look at her. And couldn't conceal his dismay at the sight of her.

Old Rit hovered over her, a prayer on her lips. Not this child, she couldn't lose this one. Two of her girls had been sold already, sold South, part of the chain gang, crying, protesting, pulling back, and the chains pulling them forward, clanking sound of the chains, cracking sound of the whip of the driver.

Old Rit nursed Harriet alone, unaided. She even called in the old man that they said could conjure, though she doubted that any conjurer in the world could save this child. At night, in the flickering light from the fire, it seemed to her that the wound, that great hole in the forehead, throbbed.

That night, in the slave cabins in the quarter, they talked about Harriet. If she lived, she would be sold South; the overseer and the master would not keep an intractable, defiant slave, a slave who refused to help the overseer tie up a runaway, blocking the door like Harriet did. She would be sold. It was a dangerous thing that she had done. Dangerous, yes, but a brave thing, too. Why wasn't she afraid? What had made her so bold? And someone spoke of Denmark Vesey: "We are slaves." And Denmark's answer: "You deserve to be!"

The cornhusking was forgotten, the fun of it, the singing, the capering that had gone on while they husked the corn.

Ghosts wandered in the quarter, whispered in the quarter. Denmark Vesey and Nat Turner haunted the Big House, too. The master couldn't sleep. He kept listening, wondering. Were they plotting something out there in the quarter? Why were they so quiet? Or were they? The air seemed to be filled with whispering voices.

Night after night the slaves kept creeping into the cabin to look at Harriet. They knew that the overseer was trying to sell her, trying to sell this dozing, half-conscious young girl, who never moved from the pallet on the floor.

November came and passed. Then it was Christmas. Harriet was in a stupor most of the time, deaf to the laughter, the dancing and the singing, deaf to the clack of the bones, the beat of the juba.

Right after Christmas the overseer began again, trying to sell her. Neighboring farmers came and looked at her and snorted their refusal to buy her; some of them laughed and said Brodas was crazy to try to sell such a wreck; others said he would have to pay them to take her off his hands, not worth a sixpence—sell her? ha! ha! ha!

Harriet stayed in the cabin from Christmas until March, and toward the end of this long period of inertness, she began to pray for the conversion of Edward Brodas, repeating the same prayer, over and over again, "Change his heart, Lord, convert him."

In March, too, when it was obvious that she was getting better, she learned that she and her brothers were to be sold South, part of the next chain gang. Austin Woodfolk, the slave trader, was in Cambridge, and Brodas had arranged for her sale.

The knowledge that she would be sold terrified her. There was always an ache in her skull, a pounding. The wound had healed but it was still painful. She was subject to violent headaches. What was worse, she never knew at what moment she would suddenly go to sleep. It was as though she lost consciousness. She never knew when this would happen or for how long a period of time. When she slept like that, she could not be roused. It was like a coma. She could remember what had gone on just before the period of unconsciousness, could pick up a conversation, the threads of it. If she was talking herself when she suddenly went to sleep, she would finish whatever she was going to say when she awakened.

But she was going to be sold. Going to be sold. She changed the prayer that she said every night. She no longer prayed for the master's conversion. She said, "Lord, if you're never going to change that man's heart—*kill him,* Lord, and take him out of the way—"

"*Kill him,* Lord!" She said it over and over again. She knew she could not survive that trip South with the chain gang, survive the slave driver's whip. She might suddenly go to sleep. She was unable to move when she went into that curious trancelike sleep. She would be beaten. She would die on the road, on that old slave road that ran straight on down into the deep South. She thought she could hear the clank of the chains, could see her brothers watching her die, unable to do anything about it.

"*Kill him,* Lord," she prayed. She knew she couldn't run away. She might be found sitting sound asleep, not a mile away from the plantation, motionless by the side of the road, in plain view.

A few days later she heard that Edward Brodas, the master, was sick, and that the doctor had told the family he would surely die. His body servant whispered the word to the mistress's personal maid, who told the kitchen help, who relayed the message to the coachman, who told one of the stable boys, who told one of the children, who ran like the wind, to tell Harriet and Old Rit. The message was transmitted mouth to ear, ear to mouth, with gestures made by swift-moving hands that showed just how sick the master was.

And then, suddenly, one morning the master was dead. The field hands knew he was dead before the overseer knew it. And no one watching them could really have said how the news spread so fast, the length and breadth of the whole plantation, though the word went from the master's bedroom, to the kitchen, then to the stable, then to the quarter, where the little children managed to tell the field hands while they brought the water to them.

It was planting time, and the backs of the field hands were bent as they leaned over the long rows, sun glistening on their bare backs. Seedtime. Seedtime.

The overseer, a man on horseback watching them, suddenly shouted, "Make a noise there!" because a hush fell over the field.

They began to sing. But it was a slow-moving song, pitched higher than anything he had ever heard, with a wail in it that made him shiver, and the words made him shiver, too:

He know moon-rise, he know star-rise,
  But he done lain his body down.

Old master'll walk in the moonlight, he'll
    walk in the starlight
  To lay his body down.

Old master'll walk in the graveyard,
He'll walk through the graveyard,
  To lay his body down.

Old master'll lie in the grave and stretch out
    his arms,
  To lay his body down.

Old Rit told Harriet that the master was dead.

She didn't need to tell her. When Harriet heard that long slow wail from the fields, she knew he was dead. She lay on the floor of the cabin, motionless, conscience-stricken, filled with horror. She believed that her prayers had killed him.

In Boston, on January 1, 1831, William Lloyd Garrison published the first issue of his antislavery newspaper, The Liberator. *The following statement appeared on the front page of the first issue:*

"I will be harsh as truth and as uncompromising as justice, on this subject [slavery]. I do not want to think or write with moderation. No! No!"

8. Minta Becomes Harriet

THERE WAS PANIC in the quarter. The master was dead. Would the slaves be sold? Would all these families be separated and scattered about the countryside? The older slaves whispered to each other, saying: "Did he free us as he promised?"

Harriet, conscience-stricken, believing that her prayers had killed Edward Brodas, ignored the fear in the voices, the faces, of the slaves. She said, later, of this period, "It appeared like I would give the world full of silver and gold, if I had it, to bring that poor soul back. . . . I would give *myself;* I would give everything!"

The slaves were quickly reassured. The overseer told them that the plantation was to remain intact. It had been willed to an heir who was too young to administer it. It would be managed by the young master's guardian, Dr. Anthony Thompson, a minister in Bucktown. According to the master's will, none of the slaves could be sold outside the state of Maryland.

This information ended the whispered, panicky conversations in the quarter. It did nothing to end Harriet's feeling of guilt. Her common sense told her that her prayers could not possibly have killed the master. Yet she was not quite certain. This incident of the master's death following so swiftly after her reiterated plea, *Kill him, Lord,* left her with the conviction that prayer was always answered.

She was uneasy, too. She knew that she was no longer regarded as a desirable slave. There was always the possibility that Dr. Thompson, once he heard the story of the way in which she had defied an overseer, would decide to sell her, lest she transmit to the other slaves the same spirit of rebellion.

Once again she toyed with the idea of running away. Somehow the urgency was gone. Old Rit and Ben were here on the plantation. So were her brothers and sisters. All of them had joyously accepted the announcement that nothing was to be changed.

But who could be certain? The master had promised to free Old Rit, but he hadn't. He had never been cruel to his slaves. But he hired them out to men who were cruel. He sold them whenever the need arose. He had tried to sell her when she was sick and worthless. No one could know what this temporary master, Doc Thompson, as he was known in Bucktown, would be like. He would probably continue the old master's practice of hiring out slaves.

She knew what it was like to be hired out. One moment she had been a laughing child, running through the woods, chasing rabbits, playing with the other small children in the quarter, and the next moment she had been picked up and taken

to the home of James Cook and set to work doing
jobs that a child should not have been expected
to do.

She would always remember Miss Susan and
the whip that she kept on the little shelf behind
her bed, always remember how desperately tired
she got because she never had enough sleep. She
could see herself a child, rocking a baby in a
cradle, rock, rock, rock; could see herself sick
with the measles, walking the length of Cook's
trap line, in winter, shivering, eyes watering. She
remembered how she had hated the scaly tails of
the muskrats, the wild smell of them, and yet did
not want to find them caught fast in the traps.

Long afterward, she said of this period in her
life, "They [the slaveholders] don't know any better,
it's the way they were brought up. 'Make the little
slaves mind you, or flog them,' was what they said
to their children, and they were brought up with
the whip in their hands. Now that wasn't the way
on all plantations; there were good masters and
mistresses, as I've heard tell, but I didn't happen to
come across any of them."

After the terrible wound in her head had healed,
she became aware of the admiration of the other
slaves. Even the old ones listened to her opinions,
deferred to her. Though Old Rit continued to
deplore the audacity, the boldness in Harriet that
made her defy an overseer, she stopped calling
her Minta or Minty. So did the others.

She was Harriet now to all of them. It was as
though the pet names, the diminutives, were no

longer suitable for a teen-aged girl who bore on her forehead a great scar, irradicable evidence of the kind of courage rarely displayed by a grown-up.

Though the wound in her head had healed, she was subject to periods of troubled sleep, she had strange dreams which recurred night after night. These dreams had a three-dimensional quality in which people and places were seen more clearly, more sharply than in her waking moments. At night, in the quarter, she described these dreams or visions, as she called them, to the other slaves. Even in the telling, something of the reality of the dream came through to the others, so that they were awed by her.

As soon as she was able to work again, Doc Thompson hired out Harriet and her father, Ben, to John Stewart, a builder. At first Harriet worked in his house, doing the housework that she despised.

There was no question but what she was well enough to work, though she sometimes had severe headaches, especially if she got very tired. Then the ache was like a pounding inside her skull. The headaches did not bother her as much as the sudden onset of that deep trancelike sleep which still occurred without warning.

Whenever she thought of running away, not so often now, the knowledge of this awful weakness stopped her. She knew that she might be found asleep by the side of the road, and brought back immediately. The deep scar on her forehead made her easily recognized.

She was afraid to leave and yet she could not bear the life she led, inside all day, sweeping and dusting, making beds, washing clothes. The house was so near the woods that she could hear the ring of the axes, hear the crash as a great tree came down.

After three months of housework, she asked Stewart, her temporary master, if she could work in the woods with the men. "I always did field work," she explained. "So I can swing a ax just like a man."

Stewart knew she was strong. He had seen her bring in big logs for the fireplaces, had once stopped to watch in unconcealed amazement as she carried a tremendous iron caldron filled with hot water from the cookhouse to a nearby stream. He did not have to pay her old master, Doc Thompson, very much for her hire because she was a woman. If she could do a man's work, felling trees, splitting logs, he'd be getting a bargain.

"We can try it," he said. "If it don't work out why you'll have to go back to cooking and cleaning."

But it did work out. Harriet was delighted. She knew that Stewart was pleased with the new arrangement for shortly afterward he allowed her to "hire her time." This was a privilege which was extended to trustworthy slaves who were good workers. It meant that Harriet could find jobs for herself, and would pay Stewart fifty or sixty dollars a year. Whatever she earned over and beyond this sum, she was allowed to keep.

She sought and found jobs that would keep her out of doors. She hauled logs, plowed fields, drove an oxcart. She became a familiar figure in the fields—a slender, muscular young woman, with her skirts looped up around her waist and a vivid bandanna tied on her head. Dressed in this fashion, she did the rough hard work of a prime field hand.

During this period, she often worked with Ben, her father. John Stewart placed Ben in charge of the slaves who cut the timber which was to be sent by boat to the Baltimore shipyard. For weeks at a time Harriet swung a broadax in the woods as part of Ben's crew, cutting half a cord of wood a day just like a man.

She learned most of the woods lore that she knew from Ben: the names of birds, which berries were good to eat and which were poisonous, where to look for water lilies, how to identify the hemlocks and the plant that he called cranebill, wild geranium or crane's bill. For these things—bark of hemlock, root of water lily, leaf of crane's bill—had medicinal value. The slaves used them to cure all sorts of ailments, fevers and intestinal disorders.

Harriet was an apt pupil. Ben said that her eyes were sharper than his. She said, "No. It's not just my eyes. It's my hands, too." She thought her hands seemed to locate the root or herb she was seeking before she actually saw it.

Ben taught her how to pick a path through the woods, even through the underbrush, without making a sound. He said, "Any old body can go through a woods crashing and mashing things down like a cow. That's easy. You practice doing it the hard way—move so quiet even a bird on a nest don't hear you and fly up."

Neither of them ever discussed the reasons why it was desirable to be able to go through the woods soundlessly. Discussion wasn't necessary. Deep inside herself Harriet knew what Ben was doing. He was, in his own fashion, training her for the day when she might become a runaway, and a successful flight would depend on the stealth of her movements through the woods that bordered all the roads.

When she was nineteen, Ben rewarded her efforts with praise. She had followed him through the woods and though he moved quietly himself, he had not heard her, although she was close behind him. When they reached a clearing, she came up in back of him and touched him lightly on the arm. He jumped, startled, and then laughed when he saw Harriet standing beside him.

He said, "Hat, you walk like a Injun. Not even a leaf make a rustle, not even a twig crack back on itself when you come through there."

She was tremendously pleased by this. She thought if only her master, John Stewart, would stop having her exhibit her strength for the entertainment of his guests, she would be content to spend the rest of her life on this plantation hiring herself out. The work was hard, yes, but now that she was grown, she could do the most backbreaking jobs without effort. Besides the workday was lightened and shortened by moments of fun, by words of praise like those of Ben's, by the endless wonder and beauty of the woods.

Unfortunately, Stewart had long since discovered that she was as strong as any of the men on the plantation. She could lift barrels of produce, could shoulder heavy timbers. Whenever he had visitors, he gave orders that she was to be hitched to a boat loaded with stone and was to drag it behind her as she walked along the edge of the river. She could hear cries of astonishment, laughter, applause from the men who stood on the bank watching. This audience of fashionably dressed planters made her feel that she was little better than a trained animal, brought out for their amusement.

Though Stewart continued to have her perform for his friends, she remained with him, hiring her time, for six years.

In Boston, on October 21, 1835, William Lloyd Garrison, publisher of The Liberator, *was rescued from a mob of some two thousand well-dressed, eminently respectable men who were intent on hanging him. The mayor and the constables got Garrison away from the crowd and finally lodged him in the Leverett Street Jail for safety.*

That night, thin, bespectacled William Lloyd Garrison wrote on the wall of his cell: "William Lloyd Garrison was put into this cell on Monday afternoon, October 21, 1835, to save him from the violence of a respectable and influential mob, who sought to destroy him for preaching the abominable and dangerous doctrine that all men are created equal, and that all oppression is odious in the sight of God."

9. The Patchwork Quilt

In 1843, Harriet Ross began to make a patchwork quilt. She had trouble finding the brilliantly colored pieces of cotton cloth she needed. Sewing the quilt together was even harder.

The needle kept slipping through her fingers. Sometimes she did not know that she had lost it, until she tried to take a stitch and found that she held only a long piece of thread. Time and again she hunted for the needle on the dirt floor of the cabin. It was difficult to find it there, difficult for fingers accustomed to grasping the handle of a broadax to pick up an object as tiny as a needle.

It seemed as though she would never be able to master the art of sewing, to make the needle go through the material in the places where she wanted it to go. It was the hardest task she had ever undertaken.

Yet as the quilt pattern developed, she thought it was as beautiful as the wild flowers that grew in the woods and along the edge of the roads. The yellow was like the Jerusalem flower, and the purple suggested motherwort, and the white pieces were like water lily, and the varying shades of green represented the leaves of all the plants, and the eternal green of the pine trees.

For this was no ordinary quilt. It would be trousseau, and the entire contents of what under different circumstances would have been a hope chest. Harriet had fallen in love. She was going to marry a young man named John Tubman. He was a tall, well-built fellow, with a ready laugh, and a clear lilting whistle.

When she worked on the quilt, head bent, awkward fingers guiding the needle carefully through the material, she experienced a strange, tender feeling that was new to her. The quilt became a symbol of the life that she would share with John. She thought about him while she sewed, how tall he was, how sweet the sound of his whistling. She was so short she had to look up to him. She looked up to him for another reason, too. He was free. He had always been free. Yet he wanted to marry her and she was a slave. So she felt humble, too.

They were married in 1844. Harriet went to live in his cabin, taking with her her one beautiful possession, the patchwork quilt.

The knowledge that she was still a slave bothered her more and more. If she were sold, she would be separated from John. She truly loved him. She had asked him how he came to be free. He said it was because his mother and father had been freed by their master, at the time of the master's death.

This made Harriet wonder about her own family, especially about Old Rit, who was forever talking about the promise of freedom that had been made to her. She paid five dollars to a lawyer to look up the wills of the various masters to whom Old Rit had belonged. It had taken her years to save five dollars, she had hoarded pennies to accumulate such a sum. But it seemed to her the information she received was well worth the cost. She found that Old Rit had originally been willed to a young woman named Mary Patterson, with the provision that she was to be freed when she was forty-five. Mary Patterson died shortly afterward, still unmarried. According to the lawyer, Old Rit should have been freed long ago. Instead she remained a slave, and so, of course, her children were slaves. Old Rit had been sold and resold many times.

After this, Harriet grew more and more discontented. She felt that she was a slave only because Old Rit had been tricked and deceived, years ago.

Times were hard the year that Harriet married John Tubman. And the next year, too. In the quarter she heard a great deal of talk about the reasons for this. One of the house servants said the trouble was due to the difference in the price of cotton. Dr. Thompson had said so. He said cotton brought thirteen cents a pound in 1837, and when it was high, the slave traders paid as much as a thousand dollars for prime field hands. Then cotton started going down, down, down, until now in 1845 it was bringing only five cents a pound, and the slave traders gave less than five hundred dollars for young strong slaves.

Harriet decided that from the dilapidated look of the plantation—fields lying fallow, the Big House in need of repair—Doc Thompson would soon be selling slaves again. He wouldn't be able to get much for them in Maryland, so in spite of the old master's will, he would sell them South.

She told John Tubman this. Every time she said it, she spoke of going North, of running away, following the North Star.

He warned her against such foolishness. What would she find there that she didn't have here? She hired her time, and so she always had a little money of her own. They had a cabin to themselves. Maryland was a good place to live. It never got too cold. There were all the coves and creeks where one could fish and set traps.

He said that if she went North, she'd freeze to death. Besides, what happened to the ones who went there? None of them came back to tell what it was like. Why was that? Because they couldn't. They died there. They must have. If they were still alive, they would have returned to show the way to some of the rest of the slaves. None returned. None sent back word. What would she have there that she didn't have here?

Her reply was always the same: "I'd be free."

She told him about the dreams she had, how night after night, she dreamed that men on horseback came riding into the quarter, and then she heard the shrieks and screams of women and children, as they were put into the chain gang, that the screaming of the women made her wake up. She would lie there in the dark of the cabin, sweating, feeling cold because the fire was out, and the chill from the dirt floor seemed to have reached her very bones, and, though awake, she could still hear the echo of screams.

When she went back to sleep she would dream again. This time she was flying. She flew over cotton fields and cornfields, and the corn was ripe, the tassels waving all golden brown in the wind, and then she flew over Cambridge and the Choptank River, and she could see the gleam of the water, like a mirror, far down, under her, and then she came to a mountain and flew over that. At last she reached a barrier, sometimes it was a fence, sometimes a river, and she couldn't fly over it.

She said, "It appeared like I wouldn't have the strength, and just as I was sinking down, there would be ladies all dressed in white over there, and they would put out their arms and pull me across—"

John Tubman disliked these dreams. When she retold them, her husky voice pitched low, she made them sound as though they had really happened. He thought this showed how restless and impatient she had become. He laughed at her, finally. He said that she must be related to Old Cudjo, who was so slow-witted he never laughed at a funny story until a half hour after it was told. Because only a slow-witted person would have the same dream all the time.

In spite of his derision, she kept telling him about her dreams. She said that on clear nights the North Star seemed to beckon to her. She was sure she could follow that star. They could go North together. Then she would be free too. Nothing could part them then.

He decided he would put an end to this talk of escape, of the North, and freedom. He asked what she would do when the sky was dark. Then how would she know which way was North? She couldn't read the signs along the road. She wouldn't know which way to go. He would not go with her. He was perfectly satisfied where he was. She would be alone, in the dark, in the silence of the deep woods. What would she eat? Where would she get food?

She started to say: in the woods. She could live a long time on the edible berries and fruit that she had long ago learned to recognize. And yet—she had seen many a half-starved runaway brought back in chains, not enough flesh left on him to provide a decent meal for a buzzard. Perhaps she, too, would starve. She remembered the time she ran away from Miss Susan's and crawled into a pigpen, remembered the squealing and grunting of the pigs, the slops thrown into the trough, and fighting with the pigs, pushing them away, to get at the trough. After four days she had been indistinguishable from the pigs, filthy, foul-smelling—and starving. So she had gone back to Miss Susan. The memory of this experience made her avoid John's eyes, not answer him.

Perhaps her silence made him angry. He may have interpreted it as evidence of her stubbornness, her willfulness, her utter disregard of all his warnings, and so made a threat which would put a stop to this crazy talk about freedom.

He shouted at her, "You take off and I'll tell the Master. I'll tell the Master right quick."

She stared at him, shocked, thinking, he couldn't, he wouldn't. If he told the master that she was missing, she would be caught before she got off the plantation. John knew what happened to runaways who were caught and brought back. Surely he would not betray his own wife.

And yet—she knew that there were slaves who had betrayed other slaves when they tried to escape. Sometimes they told because they were afraid of the master, it was always hard on the ones who were left behind. Sometimes the house servants were the betrayers, they were closest to the masters, known to be tattletales, certain to be rewarded because of their talebearing.

But John Tubman was free. And free Negroes helped the runaways. It was one of the reasons the masters disliked and distrusted them. Surely John would not deny freedom to her, when he had it himself. Perhaps he was afraid he would be held responsible for her escape, afraid the master would think John had incited her to run away. Besides, he was satisfied here, he had said so, and men disliked change, or so Old Rit had told her, saying also that women thrived on it.

Then she thought, frowning, but if a man really loved a woman, wouldn't he be willing to take risks to help her to safety? She shook her head. He must have been joking, or speaking through a sudden uncontrollable anger.

"You don't mean that," she said slowly. But he

did mean it. She could tell by the way he looked at her.

For the tall young man with the gay laugh, and the merry whistle, had been replaced by a hostile stranger, who glared at her as he said, "You just start and see."

She knew that no matter what words she might hear during the rest of her life, she would never again hear anything said that hurt like this. It was as though he had deliberately tried to kill all the trust and the love and the deep devotion she had for him.

That night as she lay beside him on the floor of the cabin, she felt that he was watching her, waiting to see if this was the night when she would try to leave.

From that night on, she was afraid of him.

In the spring of the same year, Thomas Garrett, Quaker, who since 1822 had been offering food and shelter to runaway slaves in Wilmington, Delaware, was tried and found guilty of breaking the law covering fugitive slaves. Found guilty with him was John Hunn, a stationmaster of the Underground Railroad in Middletown, Delaware, and a much younger man.

The trial was held in the May Term of the United States Court, at New Castle, before Chief Justice Taney and Judge Hall.

The fines and damages that Garrett had to pay took every dollar of his property. His household effects and all his belongings were sold at public auc-

tion. The sheriff who conducted the sale turned to Garrett and said, "Thomas, I hope you'll never be caught at this again."

Garrett, who was then sixty years old, answered: "Friend, I haven't a dollar in the world, but if thee knows a fugitive anywhere on the face of the earth who needs a breakfast, send him to me."

During the operation of the Underground Railroad, twenty-five hundred slaves passed through Garrett's "station" in Wilmington.

10. "A Glory over Everything"

ONE DAY, in 1849, when Harriet was working in the fields, near the edge of the road, a white woman wearing a faded sunbonnet went past, driving a wagon. She stopped the wagon, and watched Harriet for a few minutes. Then she spoke to her, asked her what her name was, and how she had acquired the deep scar on her forehead.

Harriet told her the story of the blow she had received when she was a girl. After that, whenever the woman saw her in the fields, she stopped to talk to her. She told Harriet that she lived on a farm, near Bucktown. Then one day she said, not looking at Harriet, but looking instead at the overseer, far off at the edge of the fields, "If you ever need any help, Harriet, ever need any help, why you let me know."

That same year the young heir to the Brodas estate died. Harriet mentioned the fact of his death to the white woman in the faded sunbonnet, the next time she saw her. She told her of the panic-stricken talk in the quarter, told her that the slaves were afraid that the master, Dr. Thompson, would start selling them. She said that Doc Thompson no longer permitted any of them to hire their time. The woman nodded her head, clucked to the horse, and drove off, murmuring, "If you ever need any help—"

The slaves were right about Dr. Thompson's intention. He began selling slaves almost immediately. Among the first ones sold were two of Harriet Tubman's sisters. They went South with the chain gang on a Saturday.

When Harriet heard of the sale of her sisters, she knew that the time had finally come when she must leave the plantation. She was reluctant to attempt the long trip North alone, not because of John Tubman's threat to betray her, but because she was afraid she might fall asleep somewhere along the way and so would be caught immediately.

She persuaded three of her brothers to go with her. Having made certain that John was asleep, she left the cabin quietly, and met her brothers at the edge of the plantation. They agreed that she was to lead the way, for she was more familiar with the woods than the others.

The three men followed her, crashing through the underbrush, frightening themselves, stopping constantly to say, "What was that?" or "Someone's coming."

She thought of Ben and how he had said, "Any old body can go through a woods crashing and mashing things down like a cow." She said sharply, "Can't you boys go quieter? Watch where you're going!"

One of them grumbled, "Can't see in the dark. Ain't got cat's eyes like you."

"You don't need cat's eyes," she retorted. "On a

night like this, with all the stars out, it's not black dark. Use your own eyes."

She supposed they were doing the best they could but they moved very slowly. She kept getting so far ahead of them that she had to stop and wait for them to catch up with her, lest they lose their way. Their progress was slow, uncertain. Their feet got tangled in every vine. They tripped over fallen logs, and once one of them fell flat on his face. They jumped, startled, at the most ordinary sounds: the murmur of the wind in the branches of the trees, the twittering of a bird. They kept turning around, looking back.

They had not gone more than a mile when she became aware that they had stopped. She turned and went back to them. She could hear them whispering. One of them called out, "Hat!"

"What's the matter? We haven't got time to keep stopping like this."

"We're going back."

"No," she said firmly. "We've got a good start. If we move fast and move quiet—"

Then all three spoke at once. They said the same thing, over and over, in frantic hurried whispers, all talking at once:

They told her that they had changed their minds. Running away was too dangerous. Someone would surely see them and recognize them. By morning the master would know they had "took off." Then the handbills advertising them would be posted all over Dorchester County. The patterollers would search for them. Even if they were lucky enough to elude the patrol, they could not possibly hide from the bloodhounds. The hounds would be baying after them, snuffing through the swamps and the underbrush, zigzagging through the deepest woods. The bloodhounds would surely find them. And everyone knew what happened to a runaway who was caught and brought back alive.

She argued with them. Didn't they know that if they went back they would be sold, if not tomorrow, then the next day, or the next? Sold South. They had seen the chain gangs. Was that what they wanted? Were they going to be slaves for the rest of their lives? Didn't freedom mean anything to them?

"You're afraid," she said, trying to shame them into action. "Go on back. I'm going North alone."

Instead of being ashamed, they became angry. They shouted at her, telling her that she was a fool and they would make her go back to the plantation with them. Suddenly they surrounded her, three men, her own brothers, jostling her, pushing her along, pinioning her arms behind her. She fought against them, wasting her strength, exhausting herself in a furious struggle.

She was no match for three strong men. She said, panting, "All right. We'll go back. I'll go with you."

She led the way, moving slowly. Her thoughts were bitter. Not one of them was willing to take a small risk in order to be free. It had all seemed so perfect, so simple, to have her brothers go with her, sharing the dangers of the trip together, just as a family should. Now if she ever went North, she would have to go alone.

Two days later, a slave working beside Harriet in the fields motioned to her. She bent toward him, listening. He said the water boy had just brought news to the field hands, and it had been passed from one to the other until it reached him. The news was that Harriet and her brothers had been sold to the Georgia trader, and that they were to be sent South with the chain gang that very night.

Harriet went on working but she knew a moment of panic. She would have to go North alone. She would have to start as soon as it was dark. She could not go with the chain gang. She might die on the way, because of those inexplicable sleeping seizures. But then she—how could she run away? She might fall asleep in plain view along the road.

But even if she fell asleep, she thought, the Lord would take care of her. She murmured a prayer, "Lord, I'm going to hold steady on to You and You've got to see me through."

Afterward, she explained her decision to run the risk of going North alone, in these words: "I had reasoned this out in my mind; there was one of two things I had a *right* to, liberty or death; if I could not have one, I would have the other; for no man should take me alive; I should fight for my liberty as long as my strength lasted, and when the time came for me to go, the Lord would let them take me."

At dusk, when the work in the fields was over,

she started toward the Big House. She had to let someone know that she was going North, someone she could trust. She no longer trusted John Tubman and it gave her a lost, lonesome feeling. Her sister Mary worked in the Big House, and she planned to tell Mary that she was going to run away, so someone would know.

As she went toward the house, she saw the master, Doc Thompson, riding up the drive on his horse. She turned aside and went toward the quarter. A field hand had no legitimate reason for entering the kitchen of the Big House—and yet—there must be some way she could leave word so that afterward someone would think about it and know that she had left a message.

As she went toward the quarter she began to sing. Dr. Thompson reined in his horse, turned around and looked at her. It was not the beauty of her voice that made him turn and watch her, frowning, it was the words of the song that she was singing, and something defiant in her manner, that disturbed and puzzled him.

When that old chariot comes,
I'm going to leave you,
I'm bound for the promised land,
Friends, I'm going to leave you.

I'm sorry, friends, to leave you,
Farewell! Oh, farewell!
But I'll meet you in the morning,
Farewell! Oh, farewell!

I'll meet you in the morning,
   When I reach the promised land;
On the other side of Jordan,
   For I'm bound for the promised land.

That night when John Tubman was asleep, and the fire had died down in the cabin, she took the ashcake that had been baked for their breakfast, and a good-sized piece of salt herring, and tied them together in an old bandanna. By hoarding this small stock of food, she could make it last a long time, and with the berries and edible roots she could find in the woods, she wouldn't starve.

She decided that she would take the quilt with her, too. Her hands lingered over it. It felt soft and warm to her touch. Even in the dark, she thought she could tell one color from another, because she knew its pattern and design so well.

Then John stirred in his sleep, and she left the cabin quickly, carrying the quilt carefully folded under her arm.

Once she was off the plantation, she took to the woods, not following the North Star, not even looking for it, going instead toward Bucktown. She needed help. She was going to ask the white woman who had stopped to talk to her so often if she would help her. Perhaps she wouldn't. But she would soon find out.

When she came to the farmhouse where the woman lived, she approached it cautiously, circling around it. It was so quiet. There was no sound at all, not even a dog barking, or the sound of voices. Nothing.

She tapped on the door, gently. A voice said, "Who's there?" She answered, "Harriet, from Dr. Thompson's place."

When the woman opened the door she did not seem at all surprised to see her. She glanced at the little bundle that Harriet was carrying, at the quilt, and invited her in. Then she sat down at the kitchen table, and wrote two names on a slip of paper, and handed the paper to Harriet.

She said that those were the next places where it was safe for Harriet to stop. The first place was a farm where there was a gate with big white posts and round knobs on top of them. The people there would feed her, and when they thought it was safe for her to go on, they would tell her how to get to the next house, or take her there. For these were the first two stops on the Underground Railroad— going North, from the Eastern Shore of Maryland.

Thus Harriet learned that the Underground Railroad that ran straight to the North was not a railroad at all. Neither did it run underground. It was composed of a loosely organized group of people who offered food and shelter, or a place of concealment, to fugitives who had set out on the long road to the North and freedom.

Harriet wanted to pay this woman who had befriended her. But she had no money. She gave her the patchwork quilt, the only beautiful object she had ever owned.

That night she made her way through the woods,

crouching in the underbrush whenever she heard the sound of horses' hoofs, staying there until the riders passed. Each time she wondered if they were already hunting for her. It would be so easy to describe her, the deep scar on her forehead like a dent, the old scars on the back of her neck, the husky speaking voice, the lack of height, scarcely five feet tall. The master would say she was wearing rough clothes when she ran away, that she had a bandanna on her head, that she was muscular and strong.

She knew how accurately he would describe her. One of the slaves who could read used to tell the others what it said on those handbills that were nailed up on the trees, along the edge of the roads. It was easy to recognize the handbills that advertised runaways, because there was always a picture in one corner, a picture of a black man, a little running figure with a stick over his shoulder, and a bundle tied on the end of the stick.

Whenever she thought of the handbills, she walked faster. Sometimes she stumbled over old grapevines, gnarled and twisted, thick as a man's wrist, or became entangled in the tough, sinewy vine of the honeysuckle. But she kept going.

In the morning, she came to the house where her friend had said she was to stop. She showed the slip of paper that she carried to the woman who answered her knock at the back door of the farmhouse. The woman fed her, and then handed her a broom and told her to sweep the yard.

Harriet hesitated, suddenly suspicious. Then she

decided that with a broom in her hand, working in the yard, she would look as though she belonged on the place, certainly no one would suspect that she was a runaway.

That night the woman's husband, a farmer, loaded a wagon with produce. Harriet climbed in. He threw some blankets over her, and the wagon started.

It was dark under the blankets, and not exactly comfortable. But Harriet decided that riding was better than walking. She was surprised at her own lack of fear, wondered how it was that she so readily trusted these strangers who might betray her. For all she knew, the man driving the wagon might be taking her straight back to the master.

She thought of those other rides in wagons, when she was a child, the same clop-clop of the horses' feet, creak of the wagon, and the feeling of being lost because she did not know where she was going. She did not know her destination this time either, but she was not alarmed. She thought of John Tubman. By this time he must have told the master that she was gone. Then she thought of the plantation and how the land rolled gently down toward the river, thought of Ben and Old Rit, and that Old Rit would be inconsolable because her favorite daughter was missing. "Lord," she prayed, "I'm going to hold steady onto You. You've got to see me through." Then she went to sleep.

The next morning when the stars were still visible in the sky, the farmer stopped the wagon. Harriet was instantly awake.

He told her to follow the river, to keep following it to reach the next place where people would take her in and feed her. He said that she must travel only at night, and she must stay off the roads because the patrol would be hunting for her. Harriet climbed out of the wagon. "Thank you," she said simply, thinking how amazing it was that there should be white people who were willing to go to such lengths to help a slave get to the North.

When she finally arrived in Pennsylvania, she had traveled roughly ninety miles from Dorchester County. She had slept on the ground outdoors at night. She had been rowed for miles up the Choptank River by a man she had never seen before. She had been concealed in a haycock, and had, at one point, spent a week hidden in a potato hole in a cabin which belonged to a family of free Negroes. She had been hidden in the attic of the home of a Quaker. She had been befriended by stout German farmers, whose guttural speech surprised her and whose well-kept farms astonished her. She had never before seen barns and fences, farmhouses and outbuildings, so carefully painted. The cattle and horses were so clean they looked as though they had been scrubbed.

When she crossed the line into the free state of Pennsylvania, the sun was coming up. She said, "I looked at my hands to see if I was the same person now I was free. There was such a glory over everything, the sun came like gold through the trees, and over the fields, and I felt like I was in heaven."

"A Glory over Everything"

In December, 1849, most of the speeches made in Congress dealt with the need for a more stringent fugitive slave law.

In January, 1850, Mr. Mason of Virginia said the existing law was inadequate: "You may as well go down into the sea and endeavor to recover from his native element a fish which had escaped from you as expect to recover a fugitive. Every difficulty is thrown in your way by the population."

Mr. Clingman of North Carolina stated that there were some 30,000 fugitives in the North—worth $15,000,000. Something must be done about it.

11. Stranger in a Strange Land

HARRIET TUBMAN's moment of exultation passed quickly. According to her own words: "There was no one to welcome me to the land of freedom. I was a stranger in a strange land, and my home after all was down in the old cabin quarter with the old folks, and my brothers and sisters."

When she thought of her family, left behind in Maryland, all of them slaves, her joy in having escaped rapidly left her. She decided that as soon as she could, she would go back to Dorchester County and lead her family North, too. She knew the way now. She knew what a fugitive would do on the nights when it rained, and the North Star was obscured. She had groped her way along, fingering the bark of trees, finding out on which side the moss grew the thickest, moving slowly from tree to tree. Her hands had been cold, and the moss was spongy and wet, the bark of the trees was rough.

But she had done it once, alone, and with the help of the Lord, she would do it again, and again, until she got all of her family out of Maryland.

That year, 1849, she went to work in a hotel in Philadelphia, as a cook. She had always hated housework. She felt trapped inside the kitchen where she worked. Yet she stayed there a year, cooking, washing dishes and pots and pans, scrubbing the floor. She saved most of the money she earned, hoarding the tips she was given. She would need money when she went back into slave territory.

At first she found Philadelphia a strange and frightening place. The streets were filled with people. There was the constant movement of horses and wagons and fine carriages. The buildings were taller than any she had ever seen. She was constantly surprised by the number of colored people that she saw, by their speech, and the fine clothes that they wore. She soon learned that many of these people were fugitive slaves like herself.

She knew moments of homesickness when she longed for the quarter, remembering the old familiar smoky smell of the cabin, the good smell of the earth when it was plowed in the spring.

Early in 1850 she visited the office of the Philadelphia Vigilance Committee. Sooner or later all fugitive slaves in the city went there seeking information about their relatives, or with requests for help of one kind or another. It was in this office, upstairs in Lebanon Seminary, that she learned the extent of the network of stops on the Underground Railroad. By 1850 the road was doing a tremendous volume of business. Philadelphia was its principal center in the East.

William Still, a Negro, was the secretary of the Vigilance Committee. J. Miller McKim, a Quaker, was the president. The Committee and its members were prepared to offer assistance to fugitives at any hour of the day or night; it might be in the form of food, clothing, money, railroad tickets, or a place to hide.

Again and again Harriet went back to the office of the Vigilance Committee. As she listened to the stories that Still told, she came to the conclusion that almost any slave who had the courage to run away was certain to reach his destination—the North. But the slaves did not know this. She decided that she would spread the word through Maryland. She herself, by accident, or intuition, or the grace of God, had come all the way from Dorchester County on the Underground Railroad—and on her own two feet. As soon as she had saved money enough to take care of any emergencies that might arise, she would go back there for her family—and anyone else who wanted to be free.

In December, 1850, she arranged for the escape of her sister, her sister's husband, John Bowley, and their two children, one of them a baby. Though John Bowley was free, his wife and children were slaves. He had learned that his family was to be sold. When he received this information, he went to a Quaker friend of his for advice and help. This man was an agent of the Underground Railroad who lived in Cambridge, Maryland.

The Quaker agent in Cambridge, knowing, as all such people did, that he was watched constantly, and that his mail might be censored, sent a message to William Still in Philadelphia. The message, which was passed along the underground route, from one person to another, said that there were two large bales of wool and two small ones that would have to be transported from Baltimore to Philadelphia. The Cambridge agent said that a small boat would be available for the shipment from Cambridge to Baltimore but he was worried about the trip from there to Philadelphia. He would, however, rely on the ingenuity of the Vigilance Committee to take care of the matter after the merchandise reached Baltimore. He pointed out that speed was absolutely essential in this undertaking.

In Philadelphia, almost every evening after work, Harriet climbed the long flight of stairs which led to a loft in the building which housed Lebanon Seminary. This served as the office for the Philadelphia Vigilance Committee. She was fascinated by the stories she heard told in that big bare room. Quite often a party of fugitive slaves arrived while she was there, and she watched William Still write their names in the big notebook that he kept, not only their names but something of their history, too.

On several occasions she had seen runaways who came from the Eastern Shore. Thus she was able to get a little thirdhand information about her father and mother, Ben and Old Rit, or about one of her brothers or sisters.

Whenever she saw any of these newly escaped slaves, she never failed to think how miraculous it was that a group of people, sometimes only one, sometimes two or three, or four, should have had the courage to start for an unknown destination without food or money or friends, with only the burning desire for freedom to keep them going. Anyone who saw them would know they were fugitives. Their clothes were torn and snagged by briars, burrs were clinging to them. They were either barefoot or their shoes were literally worn out from walking, the soles flapping, the uppers held on by string. They were startled by any unexpected sound. If there were footsteps on the long flight of stairs, or a door closed suddenly, they jumped up, trembling, nostrils distended, eyes wide open.

One night, a quiet night there, in the loft, William Still was talking to J. Miller McKim, and to Harriet, when a stranger entered the office. He nodded to Harriet and then went over to the desk where he carried on a low-voiced conversation with Still and McKim.

Suddenly Still beckoned to Harriet. "Maybe you can help us find a woman to—" Then he interrupted himself. "There's a man named—" Even though no outsider could have overhead him, he lowered his voice, "Named John Bowley—"

"Bowley?" Harriet said. "John Bowley? Where's he from?"

"From Cambridge, Maryland. And—"

"Why that's my brother-in-law," she said, excitement in her voice. "He's married to my sister Mary —and—why he's a free man. What's the trouble?"

"Yes, he's free," said Still. "But his wife and children are slaves. And they are about to be sold. We know how to get them to Baltimore. But we've got to find someone to guide them from Baltimore to Philadelphia, preferably a woman, because there's a baby and another child. We thought you might know of a woman who would—"

"I will," she said promptly.

But Mr. Still shook his head. He said that it was difficult for free Negroes with all their papers in order to leave Baltimore. For her to attempt to bring them out when she was a fugitive herself would be an impossibility. They would be weighed, measured, at the railroad station or at the dock, and this information would be compared with the descriptions of all other known runaways. Even if this family bore no resemblance to any other fugitives, they still could not leave until they had obtained a bond signed by two well-known residents.

Harriet laughed. "Mr. Still, you're trying to scare me. And I don't scare easy. Besides, I know enough about the Underground Railroad now so that I know you don't have to go through any weighing and measuring to get a group of people out of Baltimore. That's my sister and her husband and her children and I'm the one that's going to Baltimore to get them."

William Still threw up his hands. "All right," he said, "but please, please, be careful."

On the morning that a message arrived saying that all the necessary, careful arrangements had been completed, John Bowley's wife and two children had been already picked up with a group of slaves and placed in the slave pen at the Courthouse in Cambridge. The auction had started that morning with the sale of prime field hands. No one showed any interest in purchasing the women and children in the lot.

At noon the auctioneer called a recess. He said that he would put the females on the block later on in the day, and went off to the inn to get his dinner. He paused a moment in the doorway and grumbled to the guard, "Much good it will do to put 'em up. Not much interest in 'em."

Meanwhile John Bowley and his Quaker friend had evolved a plan, a bold and desperate plan, which might or might not work.

Shortly after the auctioneer went to the inn, John entered the courthouse, carrying a large white official-looking envelope. He handed it to the guard who stood near the slave pen, and said, "It's a message from my master, the auctioneer. He wants me to bring that woman and the two children over to the inn." He gestured toward his family. "He thinks he's got a buyer for them."

The guard opened the envelope, read the message, nodded his head. Then because John extended his hand, he handed the envelope and the note back to him. Opening the gate of the pen, he went inside. "Get along there now," he said, pushing the woman and her two children out, separating them from the others.

John walked down the street beside them, still holding the envelope as though it were a talisman. They moved slowly. His wife was carrying the baby and the small child walked beside her, holding on to her skirts. It seemed to him they crawled along the street, and he wanted to run, to urge them to run, and, of course, dared not. He ignored his wife's questions.

There was despair in her voice as she said, "What does it mean? Why are *you* taking us to be sold? Oh, John. How could you?"

"Hush," he said, sternly. "Don't talk. You've just got to trust me."

It was noon so there was no one on the street. The town seemed asleep in the cold sunlight. He supposed folks were all in their houses eating, even the children. He kept thinking that it ought to take the auctioneer about two hours to eat and drink and talk up the afternoon's sale. He crossed the street with his family, still moving slowly, breathing hard, appalled at his own daring. But it was either this—doing what he had done—or lose his wife and children, for good.

Halfway down the street, he paused, looked back. The street was empty. "Quick, now!" he said. He opened the gate of a picket fence in front of one of the big houses. "Hurry, hurry!" he said, urging them to go faster, around the side of the house, to the back door. As they approached the door it opened for them.

His Quaker friend said, "Thee made it, John, with the help of the Lord, as I knew thee would."

They stayed in the attic of the house until dark. Then they went downstairs to the kitchen where they were fed. After they finished eating, the Quaker

led them out of the house. There was a farmer's
wagon in the dooryard. They climbed in, lay on
the floor of the wagon. Blankets were thrown over
them.

It was not a long ride but it was a jouncy one.
When the wagon stopped and the driver got down
and threw the blankets back, John knew he was
near the river, he could smell it.

All of them got in a rowboat at the edge of the
river. The driver of the wagon rowed them out to
a small fishing boat where John Bowley and his
family embarked for Baltimore.

There was food on the boat and blankets, and
he knew where he was going, knew how to sail a
boat, knew that he would be met by someone, and
yet he was vaguely uneasy. The children went to
sleep quickly. He and his wife talked, not a lot, just
now and then. If it weren't for the feeling of uncertainty, pinprick of fear, he would have enjoyed
sailing up the Chesapeake on this cold starry night.
He was sailing without lights, and so was more
aware of the night than he had ever been. He could
smell fish from the boat, could see lights from
other boats.

He had been told that when he got near Baltimore, he was to watch for two lights, close together,
a yellow one and a blue one. When he saw them
he was to get in the dinghy and row to them. He
kept worrying about it. Suppose he missed the
lights, suppose—

Toward morning there was faint color in the sky,
not really daylight, a lifting of the darkness. He

kept peering at the shore. Suddenly he saw the lights, a yellow one and a blue one, and sailed toward them. He got his wife and children in the dinghy and rowed shoreward.

As he drew nearer he saw where the lights came from—two barn lanterns, the shades tinted, one blue and the other yellow. There was a wagon quite close to the shore in a wooded area, a bent-over figure on the seat. To his surprise he saw that it was a woman, a white woman, tremendously fat, who turned and watched him as he got out of the boat.

"Who are you?" she asked.

At first he could only whisper. For he did not know what to expect. Then he said, "A friend with friends." That was the password he had been told to use.

"God bless you, you made it," she said. "I've been watching for two mornings straight."

Then she started moving quickly for so large a woman. The wagon held potatoes and onions, not many of them, but quite a few. She rearranged the load. John and his wife lay down in the back of the wagon with the small child, and the fat woman took the baby and held it in her arms, then wrapped it loosely under the shawl she wore over her coat.

John thought, She's so big nobody'd know that the baby was there.

The woman said, "I got to cover you up," and threw blankets over them.

Again it was a long jouncy ride. When the wagon stopped they were in the yard of a stable, and it was broad daylight. They stayed inside the stable all that day. The fat woman said she'd be back for them that night, and she gave them a package of food. They ate quickly, hungrily. Then they just sat waiting for night.

When it was dark the woman came for them. They climbed in the wagon again. This time they only went a short distance. The fat woman helped them out of the wagon, guided them toward the back door of a brick house. She tapped lightly at the door. Someone opened it. They all went inside.

John looked at the short stocky figure standing in the middle of the big warm kitchen. It was a man, a stranger, and yet—he thought the face was familiar. Then his wife said, laughing, "Harriet! It's Harriet!"

"A friend with friends," she said and chuckled.

They stayed in the house in Baltimore for a week. After that Harriet, fearless, self-assured, guided them from one station stop to the next. At each house, word was sent on to the next stop to be on the alert, to watch for this party of fugitives. Thus Harriet became aware of a new undercurrent of fear all along the route.

When she reached Philadelphia with her passengers, she took them straight to the office of the Philadelphia Vigilance Committee. There the talk was about the new Fugitive Slave Law, now three months old, and what it would mean to people like herself and to the people who offered them shelter. People convicted of harboring slaves could be imprisoned or fined so heavily that they would lose everything they owned. As for the runaways, they might be shot out of hand, or whipped and sold to the deep South, where they would die anyway. It was this that had created the undercurrent of fear.

The Fugitive Slave Law was one of the concessions made to the South as part of the Compromise of 1850. Henry Clay, John C. Calhoun and Daniel Webster believed that this compromise would heal the rapidly growing breach between the North and the South. Actually it only served to widen it, primarily because of the terms of the new law covering fugitive slaves.

In the North, men who had been indifferent to slavery, men who had been openly hostile toward the Abolitionists, men who hated Garrison and his newspaper, The Liberator, *with a deep and abiding hatred, were stirred to anger. They said that the new law turned them into slave catchers. They said they would not lift so much as a finger to help Southern slaveowners catch their runaways. Even more important, they began to question the logic of the Southern apologists for slavery. They said that if enslaved Negroes enjoyed all the good things of life that their masters said they did, there would be no runaway slaves. Why, then, were they taking to their heels in such numbers that it was necessary to pass a law to compel them to enjoy the benefits they derived from slavery?*

12. Freedom's Clothes

LIKE OTHER runaway slaves, Harriet Tubman was no longer safe in Philadelphia. Because of the Fugitive Slave Law she was liable to be arrested at any moment even though she was living in a free state. It was now doubly dangerous for her to return to slave territory, yet in the spring of 1851 she went back to Dorchester County. She brought away one of her brothers and two other men, and got them safely through to Philadelphia.

That summer she worked in Cape May, New Jersey, in a hotel. She saved practically all of her earnings, living like a miser, hoarding each penny. She planned to go back to Maryland in the fall and she would need money to finance the trip.

This was to be a special trip with only one purpose behind it: to persuade John Tubman to go North with her. It had been two years since she had seen him. During that time she had not only forgiven him for his threat to betray her, but she had begun to remember all the things about him that had made her fall in love with him: his easy laughter, his sense of humor, the tall broad-shouldered build of him.

And so one night, in the fall of 1851, she arrived at the plantation again. She lingered in the woods, on the edge of the fields, impatiently anticipating the moment when she would see John face to face. The Big House was mellow with light, and in a sense, so were the cabins in the quarter, for the flickering light from the fireplaces showed through the doorways—soft, yellowish.

She was wearing a man's suit, a man's felt hat on her head. She felt perfectly safe, confident. She knew that the master, Dr. Thompson, would not expect her to return to the plantation from which she had once managed to escape. Besides, she had been back here before.

Her knowledge of the route was so sure that she could go North rapidly now, knowing all the stops along the way, where it was safe to spend the night, which houses would provide a warm welcome. With this knowledge she could easily refute all of John's arguments about the dangers involved for those who ran away.

Late that night she went toward the cabin where she had lived with John Tubman, knocked softly. She heard the murmur of voices. Then John opened the door. At first she saw only his face, the familiar beloved face that she had for weeks now longed to see again. She had forgotten how tall he was—how broad his shoulders.

She held out her hands, smiling at him. He simply stared at her. She remembered the man's suit, the old felt hat, and she said, chuckling, "It's Harriet."

For the first time she noticed that he was not alone in the cabin. A woman got up from a stool near the fireplace, and came and stood beside him.

She was young, slender, infinitely more attractive than Harriet.

Harriet tried to explain why she had come back but the words did not come easily. She felt like an outsider, a stranger. She was terribly aware of the man's suit, the burrs clinging to it, the material old and worn and snagged by briars, the man's shoes on her feet, the battered old hat. These two people standing there, side by side, silhouetted in the doorway, light from the fireplace behind them, seemed to belong in the cabin. Something in their posture suggested that she did not, that she was an intruder.

She spoke of the North, and how they could live there together, and possibly have children. There was a yearning tenderness in her voice. She said, "I came back for you, John."

"Me?" he said, and put his arm around the young woman. "This is Caroline," he said. "Caroline is my wife now. I'm not going North or anywhere else. I wouldn't leave here for nothing in the world." Then he laughed.

Harriet had wanted to hear him laugh again, hear that happy carefree laughter of his. But not this way. She hated the sound of it. It was mocking laughter, and the woman standing there beside him was laughing, too.

She lifted her head proudly. She would never let either of them know that a world had collapsed for her, a dream had been destroyed.

"John!" she said. "Oh, John—" pleading, desperate.

How wrong she had been to make plans for him. Why had she assumed that he would be willing to go North with her when he had refused before? She had forgotten that she had always been imbued with the idea of freedom, magic in the very sound of the word, and he had always been indifferent to it, perhaps because he possessed it himself. She thought with something like contempt he should have been a slave—he deserves to be one. She compared him with John Bowley, her brother-in-law, who was willing to risk his own life and safety, though he was a free man, in order that his wife and children should not be slaves.

She remembered how she had dreamed of living in Philadelphia with John Tubman. She wanted to plead with him. Then she knew a moment of anger and wanted to shout at them because she felt they had cheated her out of her dream, defrauded her. She hated this young woman who was now leaning against John, the look of puzzlement now replaced by disdain.

She thought, If only she had been wearing fine clothes, silk or satin instead of the torn shabby suit. Not silk or velvet, just a simple calico dress, a dress that would have immediately revealed that she was a woman. Then she shook her head. How could she sleep on the ground in a dress, climb in and out of a potato hole in long skirts? Besides, clothes did not change a person, did not really matter. Love and devotion should not depend on the kind of clothes one wore. A man's suit or a woman's dress would not have made one whit of difference. Neither the one nor the other could alter or change the kind of person that she was. Her mind, her soul, would always wear freedom's clothes. John's never would.

And yet—"I came back for you, John," she said again.

John and the woman laughed. Harriet stood there for a moment, wanting to cry. She thought of the long way she had come, of the money she had earned doing the housework that she hated, remembered how for months she had condemned him in her mind as worthless, and how that judgment had been softened by time, until she had remembered only the good in him, re-experiencing in retrospect the moments of warmth, of understanding, remembering how she had made the colorful quilt, dreaming about him like any young engaged girl. When she made the quilt, she was transformed. The field hand felling trees, cutting half a cord of wood a day, lifting barrels of flour, pulling loaded boats along the edge of the river like a horse, had been turned into a girl in love, melting with tenderness.

Even now she found it impossible to hate him. She was too much in love with him. But there was an emptiness, vast, unfillable, inside of her. It would stay with her forever.

Suddenly she remembered his previous threat. It wasn't safe to stay here. He might betray her. He had always said that he would.

She turned away, taking with her the memory

of John Tubman and the young woman, Caroline, who had replaced her in his life.

By midnight she had collected a small group of slaves, all of whom wanted to be free, and started North with them, heading for Philadelphia.

The Reverend Theodore Parker, who when a boy bought a Latin dictionary with the first money he ever earned, was chairman of the Executive Committee of the Boston Vigilance Committee. On November 21, 1850, he wrote a letter to Millard Fillmore, who was then President of the United States. In the letter he not only expressed his own conviction that the Fugitive Slave Law was wrong, but he eloquently expressed the refusal of the Abolitionists to obey the law:

". . . I am not a man who loves violence; I respect the sacredness of human life, but this I say, solemnly, that I will do all in my power to rescue any fugitive slave from the hands of any officer who attempts to return him to bondage. . . . I will do it as readily as I would lift a man out of the water, or pluck him from the teeth of a wolf, or snatch him from the hands of a murderer. What is a fine of a thousand dollars, and gaoling for six months, to the liberty of a man? *My money perish with me if it stand between me and the eternal law of God!*"

13. The Legend of Moses

UP UNTIL the time of Harriet's discovery of John Tubman's infidelity, she had been guiding escaping slaves to the North and freedom largely because she wanted to rescue members of her own family. It is true that in each group she had conducted there were people who were not related to her, but the motive that had inspired the trips was always the same: to guide her own relatives into the free state of Pennsylvania.

After she discovered that John had found happiness with another woman, she brought a group of slaves North with her, none of whom was related to her. This was an unplanned, spur-of-the-moment project for she had gone back to the plantation in order to persuade her husband to go North with her. This was in keeping with the purpose behind the other trips—freedom for herself, then for her family, and, as her longing for John grew, a happy life for both of them in the North.

During the next few months, she developed a much broader purpose. She pondered over the shocking contrast between the life of a field hand in Dorchester County, Maryland, and the life she had known and enjoyed in Philadelphia and in Cape May, New Jersey. The work she had done in hotels was play compared to the terrible labors she had performed as a slave. She was free to change jobs for any reason—or for no reason at all. She could go anywhere in Philadelphia, without a pass, and no one would question her. The money that she earned was hers—all of it, to spend as she pleased or to save. To a woman who had been a slave, these were some of the great, incredible wonders of freedom. She felt that all men should enjoy these same rights and privileges.

Like the Abolitionists, she believed slavery to be morally wrong—for masters and slaves alike. She knew that she could not hope to end this evil by herself but she thought she might help make the ownership of slaves unprofitable in the area she knew so well, the Eastern Shore of Maryland. She was certain that even timid, frightened slaves would run away if someone they could trust offered to guide them to the North. She decided to keep going back to "the land of Egypt," as she called Maryland, bringing more and more away. She would leave directions for the bold, self-assured ones, drawing maps for them on the dirt floor of the cabins, carefully describing the stopping places on the route, so that they could make the trip North without a conductor. Thus she could slowly, steadily, increase the number of runaways from that one area.

Up until 1851, she was either unaware of the danger posed by the Fugitive Slave Law, or else she ignored it. But that year the significance of the new law was brought home to her, in terms of people. In Philadelphia, she heard stories about

113

three different runaways who had run afoul of the law, for these stories were being told everywhere —North and South.

The first alarming story she heard was about a runaway named Shadrach. He was arrested in Boston, on February 15, 1851, charged with being a fugitive slave. He was taken before a Federal Commissioner in the United States Courtroom for a hearing. A great crowd collected to hear the case, for this was the first test of the new law in Boston. The hearing had barely started when the Commissioner adjourned the court, to the great surprise of the people who were present.

The crowd began to leave the courtroom, moving slowly. Suddenly a group of colored men came into the room, walked over to Shadrach, and surrounded him. One of them said to him, "Follow me." Shadrach, the runaway slave, was outside the courthouse before the police officers, who were guarding him, were aware that they had just watched an impromptu and wonderfully effective rescue party at work.

Shadrach was hidden in Boston. When the search for him had ended, the Boston Vigilance Committee sent him on to Canada via the Underground Railroad.

Harriet was upset by this story, in spite of its happy ending. She had always thought of Boston as a safe place, a haven, for runaway slaves, just like Philadelphia.

Then in April, of that same year, she heard talk about a boy named Thomas Sims. He was walking along a street in Boston on the night of April 3, 1851, when he was arrested. George Ticknor Curtis, the United States Commissioner, who presided at the hearing, decided that Sims, who was a fugitive slave, must be returned to his owner in Georgia. The pro-slavery crowd in the courtroom cheered, pleased with the decision. But the Abolitionists were appalled, and talked of rescuing Sims.

But rescue was impossible. The courthouse was surrounded by a heavy chain and patrolled by a strong police force.

Sims was the first slave to be sent back into slavery by Massachusetts since the Revolution. He reached Savannah, Georgia, on the 19th, aboard the brig *Acorn*, which was owned in Boston, and had been chartered by the United States Government for the express purpose of returning the fugitive to his master.

Harriet kept hearing about Thomas Sims: That when he reached Savannah he was publicly whipped and then imprisoned for two months. After that he was sold and resold, first in Savannah, then in Charleston, then in New Orleans. He was finally taken to Vicksburg. (In 1863 when the Federal Army was besieging Vicksburg, Thomas Sims was one of the slaves who managed to reach the Federal forces. He was shipped North where he was hailed as a hero and as a prize of war.)

At first Harriet could not believe it possible that anyone could be taken out of the free state of Massachusetts and sent back to a slave state. The more she thought about it, the more it disturbed her.

The third story that Harriet Tubman heard about in Philadelphia that year concerned the slave Jerry, who was arrested in Syracuse, New York, on October 1, 1851. On that same day the Liberty Party was holding a convention in Syracuse. The delegates, having attended the morning session of the convention, had adjourned for dinner. While they were eating, they heard the slow tolling of the big bell on a nearby Congregational church.

Syracuse was an Abolitionist stronghold, and the church bells were used to give the alarm whenever a fugitive was in danger. The news spread quickly that Jerry had been arrested and was being held in the courthouse for a hearing. The streets were soon filled with men, women, children, dogs, all excited, all heading for the place where Jerry was held.

That night a group of men battered down the door of the courthouse, using a twenty-foot log. Men armed with axes and crowbars forced their way to the second floor. The Marshal fired at them, and then jumped out of a window, his arm broken. The deputies left just as hastily. Jerry was taken out of his cell by his rescuers and finally sent to Canada and freedom, via the Underground Railroad.

Harriet Tubman heard the stories about the rescue of Shadrach, and of Jerry, about the return of Thomas Sims to Georgia, talked about, told and retold. These stories showed her exactly what the new law meant to runaway slaves living anywhere in the United States, and that, of course, included her. Yet she decided that she would not permit this new and stringent law to interfere with her plan to keep guiding slaves out of Dorchester County. It was now a well-known way. She recognized every creek and cove and inlet, every neck of land, every hiding place, every curve in the roads, every potential source of danger, every potential source of safety. She knew the people who lived in the farmhouses, knew which ones would welcome her and offer food and a night's lodging, knew which ones would set after her with guns and hounds.

But the next trip she made could not end in Philadelphia. Her passengers, as she called the fugitives who would travel with her, would not be safe there, would not be safe in Boston or in Syracuse—or anywhere else in the United States. She would have to take them all the way to Canada. It would be a long trip, longer than any she had ever made, through territory that was strange and new to her, with the known hazard of the Fugitive Slave Law pacing her every footstep.

Though she was not aware of it, she had become a legend in the slave cabins along the Eastern Shore. She had always had the makings of a legend in her: the prodigious strength, the fearlessness, the religious ardor, the visions she had in which she experienced moments of prescience. Stories about her would be handed down from one generation to the next, embroidered, embellished, until it would be impossible to say which part was truth, which part was fiction. But each one who heard the stories, each one who told all of them, or only parts of them, would feel stronger because of her existence.

Pride in her would linger on in the teller of the story as well as the listener. Their faith in a living God would be strengthened, their faith in themselves would be renewed.

The slaves said she could see in the dark like a mule, that she could smell danger down the wind like a fox, that she could move through thick underbrush without making a sound, like a field mouse. They said she was so strong she could pick up a grown man, sling him over her shoulder and walk with him for miles.

They said, voices muted, awed, that she talked with God every day, just like Moses. They said there was some strange power in her so that no one could die when she was with them. She enveloped the sick and the dying with her strength, sending it from her body to theirs, sustaining them.

They changed her name again. At first she had been called Minta or Minty. After her defiance of the overseer, they called her Harriet, because the pet names, the diminutives, were no longer fitting for a girl who had displayed such courage.

Now they called her Moses.

As a result of what would always be known as the Jerry rescue, twenty-four eminently respectable citizens of Syracuse (including Reverend J. W. Loguen, Samuel May, Charles Wheaton) and Gerrit Smith, who was visiting the city, were arrested and charged with "constructive treason." The district attorney ordered them to Auburn for questioning. In Auburn, William H. Seward, later Lincoln's

Secretary of State, was one of the first men to sign the bond that had to be posted. The case dragged along for a year, and the charge was finally dropped.

14. The Railroad Runs to Canada

ALONG THE Eastern Shore of Maryland, in Dorchester County, in Caroline County, the masters kept hearing whispers about the man named Moses, who was running off slaves. At first they did not believe in his existence. The stories about him were fantastic, unbelievable. Yet they watched for him. They offered rewards for his capture.

They never saw him. Now and then they heard whispered rumors to the effect that he was in the neighborhood. The woods were searched. The roads were watched. There was never anything to indicate his whereabouts. But a few days afterward, a goodly number of slaves would be gone from the plantation. Neither the master nor the overseer had heard or seen anything unusual in the quarter. Sometimes one or the other would vaguely remember having heard a whippoorwill call somewhere in the woods, close by, late at night. Though it was the wrong season for whippoorwills.

Sometimes the masters thought they had heard the cry of a hoot owl, repeated, and would remember having thought that the intervals between the low moaning cry were wrong, that it had been repeated four times in succession instead of three. There was never anything more than that to sug-

120

gest that all was not well in the quarter. Yet when morning came, they invariably discovered that a group of the finest slaves had taken to their heels.

Unfortunately, the discovery was almost always made on a Sunday. Thus a whole day was lost before the machinery of pursuit could be set in motion. The posters offering rewards for the fugitives could not be printed until Monday. The men who made a living hunting for runaway slaves were out of reach, off in the woods with their dogs and their guns, in pursuit of four-footed game, or they were in camp meetings saying their prayers with their wives and families beside them.

Harriet Tubman could have told them that there was far more involved in this matter of running off slaves than signaling the would-be runaways by imitating the call of a whippoorwill, or a hoot owl, far more involved than a matter of waiting for a clear night when the North Star was visible.

In December, 1851, when she started out with the band of fugitives that she planned to take to Canada, she had been in the vicinity of the plantation for days, planning the trip, carefully selecting the slaves that she would take with her.

She had announced her arrival in the quarter by singing the forbidden spiritual—"Go down, Moses, 'way down to Egypt Land"—singing it softly outside the door of a slave cabin, late at night. The husky voice was beautiful even when it was barely more than a murmur borne on the wind.

Once she had made her presence known, word of her coming spread from cabin to cabin. The slaves whispered to each other, ear to mouth, mouth to ear, "Moses is here." "Moses has come." "Get ready. Moses is back again." The ones who had agreed to go North with her put ashcake and salt herring in an old bandanna, hastily tied it into a bundle, and then waited patiently for the signal that meant it was time to start.

There were eleven in this party, including one of her brothers and his wife. It was the largest group that she had ever conducted, but she was determined that more and more slaves should know what freedom was like.

She had to take them all the way to Canada. The Fugitive Slave Law was no longer a great many incomprehensible words written down on the country's lawbooks. The new law had become a reality. It was Thomas Sims, a boy, picked up on the streets of Boston at night and shipped back to Georgia. It was Jerry and Shadrach, arrested and jailed with no warning.

She had never been in Canada. The route beyond Philadelphia was strange to her. But she could not let the runaways who accompanied her know this. As they walked along she told them stories of her own first flight, she kept painting vivid word pictures of what it would be like to be free.

But there were so many of them this time. She knew moments of doubt when she was half-afraid, and kept looking back over her shoulder, imagining that she heard the sound of pursuit. They would certainly be pursued. Eleven of them. Eleven thousand dollars' worth of flesh and bone and muscle that belonged to Maryland planters. If they were caught, the eleven runaways would be whipped and sold South, but she—she would probably be hanged.

They tried to sleep during the day but they never could wholly relax into sleep. She could tell by the positions they assumed, by their restless movements. And they walked at night. Their progress was slow. It took them three nights of walking to reach the first stop. She had told them about the place where they would stay, promising warmth and good food, holding these things out to them as an incentive to keep going.

When she knocked on the door of a farmhouse, a place where she and her parties of runaways had always been welcome, always been given shelter and plenty to eat, there was no answer. She knocked again, softly. A voice from within said, "Who is it?" There was fear in the voice.

She knew instantly from the sound of the voice that there was something wrong. She said, "A friend with friends," the password on the Underground Railroad.

The door opened, slowly. The man who stood in the doorway looked at her coldly, looked with unconcealed astonishment and fear at the eleven disheveled runaways who were standing near her. Then he shouted, "Too many, too many. It's not safe. My place was searched last week. It's not safe!" and slammed the door in her face.

She turned away from the house, frowning. She had promised her passengers food and rest and warmth, and instead of that, there would be hunger and cold and more walking over the frozen ground. Somehow she would have to instill courage into these eleven people, most of them strangers, would have to feed them on hope and bright dreams of freedom instead of the fried pork and corn bread and milk she had promised them.

They stumbled along behind her, half-dead for sleep, and she urged them on, though she was as tired and as discouraged as they were. She had never been in Canada but she kept painting wondrous word pictures of what it would be like. She managed to dispel their fear of pursuit, so that they would not become hysterical, panic-stricken. Then she had to bring some of the fear back, so that they would stay awake and keep walking though they drooped with sleep.

Yet during the day, when they lay down deep in a thicket, they never really slept, because if a twig snapped or the wind sighed in the branches of a pine tree, they jumped to their feet, afraid of their own shadows, shivering and shaking. It was very cold, but they dared not make fires because someone would see the smoke and wonder about it.

She kept thinking, eleven of them. Eleven thousand dollars' worth of slaves. And she had to take them all the way to Canada. Sometimes she told them about Thomas Garrett, in Wilmington. She said he was their friend even though he did not know them. He was the friend of all fugitives. He called them God's poor. He was a Quaker and his speech was a little different from that of other people. His clothing was different, too. He wore the wide-brimmed hat that the Quakers wear.

She said that he had thick white hair, soft, almost like a baby's, and the kindest eyes she had ever seen. He was a big man and strong, but he had never used his strength to harm anyone, always to help people. He would give all of them a new pair of shoes. Everybody. He always did. Once they reached his house in Wilmington, they would be safe. He would see to it that they were.

She described the house where he lived, told them about the store where he sold shoes. She said he kept a pail of milk and a loaf of bread in the drawer of his desk so that he would have food ready at hand for any of God's poor who should suddenly appear before him, fainting with hunger. There was a hidden room in the store. A whole wall swung open, and behind it was a room where he could hide fugitives. On the wall there were shelves filled with small boxes—boxes of shoes—so that you would never guess that the wall actually opened.

While she talked, she kept watching them. They did not believe her. She could tell by their expressions. They were thinking. New shoes, Thomas Garrett, Quaker, Wilmington—what foolishness was this? Who knew if she told the truth? Where was she taking them anyway?

That night they reached the next stop—a farm that belonged to a German. She made the runaways take shelter behind trees at the edge of the fields before she knocked at the door. She hesitated before she approached the door, thinking, suppose that he, too, should refuse shelter, suppose— Then she thought, Lord, I'm going to hold steady on to You and You've got to see me through—and knocked softly.

She heard the familiar guttural voice say, "Who's there?"

She answered quickly, "A friend with friends."

He opened the door and greeted her warmly. "How many this time?" he asked.

"Eleven," she said and waited, doubting, wondering.

He said, "Good. Bring them in."

He and his wife fed them in the lamplit kitchen, their faces glowing, as they offered food and more food, urging them to eat, saying there was plenty for everybody, have more milk, have more bread, have more meat.

They spent the night in the warm kitchen. They really slept, all that night and until dusk the next day. When they left, it was with reluctance. They had all been warm and safe and well-fed. It was hard to exchange the security offered by that clean warm kitchen for the darkness and the cold of a December night.

15. "Go On or Die"

HARRIET HAD FOUND it hard to leave the warmth
and friendliness, too. But she urged them on. For
a while, as they walked, they seemed to carry in
them a measure of contentment; some of the seren-
ity and the cleanliness of that big warm kitchen
lingered on inside them. But as they walked farther
and farther away from the warmth and the light,
the cold and the darkness entered into them. They
fell silent, sullen, suspicious. She waited for the
moment when some one of them would turn muti-
nous. It did not happen that night.

Two nights later she was aware that the feet behind her were moving slower and slower. She heard
the irritability in their voices, knew that soon someone would refuse to go on.

She started talking about William Still and the
Philadelphia Vigilance Committee. No one com-
mented. No one asked any questions. She told them
the story of William and Ellen Craft and how they
escaped from Georgia. Ellen was so fair that she
looked as though she were white, and so she dressed
up in a man's clothing and she looked like a
wealthy young planter. Her husband, William, who
was dark, played the role of her slave. Thus they
traveled from Macon, Georgia, to Philadelphia,

riding on the trains, staying at the finest hotels. Ellen pretended to be very ill—her right arm was in a sling, and her right hand was bandaged, because she was supposed to have rheumatism. Thus she avoided having to sign the register at the hotels for she could not read or write. They finally arrived safely in Philadelphia, and then went on to Boston.

No one said anything. Not one of them seemed to have heard her.

She told them about Frederick Douglass, the most famous of the escaped slaves, of his eloquence, of his magnificent appearance. Then she told them of her own first vain effort at running away, evoking the memory of that miserable life she had led as a child, reliving it for a moment in the telling.

But they had been tired too long, hungry too long, afraid too long, footsore too long. One of them suddenly cried out in despair, "Let me go back. It is better to be a slave than to suffer like this in order to be free."

She carried a gun with her on these trips. She had never used it—except as a threat. Now as she aimed it, she experienced a feeling of guilt, remembering that time, years ago, when she had prayed for the death of Edward Brodas, the Master, and then not too long afterward had heard that great wailing cry that came from the throats of the field hands, and knew from the sound that the Master was dead.

One of the runaways said, again, "Let me go back. Let me go back," and stood still, and then turned around and said, over his shoulder, "I am going back."

She lifted the gun, aimed it at the despairing slave. She said, "Go on with us or die." The husky low-pitched voice was grim.

He hesitated for a moment and then he joined the others. They started walking again. She tried to explain to them why none of them could go back to the plantation. If a runaway returned, he would turn traitor, the master and the overseer would force him to turn traitor. The returned slave would disclose the stopping places, the hiding places, the cornstacks they had used with the full knowledge of the owner of the farm, the name of the German farmer who had fed them and sheltered them. These people who had risked their own security to help runaways would be ruined, fined, imprisoned.

She said, "We got to go free or die. And freedom's not bought with dust."

This time she told them about the long agony of the Middle Passage on the old slave ships, about the black horror of the holds, about the chains and the whips. They too knew these stories. But she wanted to remind them of the long hard way they had come, about the long hard way they had yet to go. She told them about Thomas Sims, the boy picked up on the streets of Boston and sent back to Georgia. She said when they got him back to Savannah, got him in prison there, they whipped him until a doctor who was standing by watching said, "You will kill him if you strike him again!" His master said, "Let him die!"

Thus she forced them to go on. Sometimes she thought she had become nothing but a voice speaking in the darkness, cajoling, urging, threatening. Sometimes she told them things to make them laugh, sometimes she sang to them, and heard the eleven voices behind her blending softly with hers, and then she knew that for the moment all was well with them.

She gave the impression of being a short, muscular, indomitable woman who could never be defeated. Yet at any moment she was liable to be seized by one of those curious fits of sleep, which might last for a few minutes or for hours.

Even on this trip, she suddenly fell asleep in the woods. The runaways, ragged, dirty, hungry, cold, did not steal the gun as they might have, and set off by themselves, or turn back. They sat on the ground near her and waited patiently until she awakened. They had come to trust her implicitly, totally. They, too, had come to believe her repeated statement, "We got to go free or die." She was leading them into freedom, and so they waited until she was ready to go on.

Finally, they reached Thomas Garrett's house in Wilmington, Delaware. Just as Harriet had promised, Garrett gave them all new shoes, and provided carriages to take them on to the next stop.

By slow stages they reached Philadelphia, where William Still hastily recorded their names, and the plantations whence they had come, and something of the life they had led in slavery. Then he carefully hid what he had written, for fear it might be discovered. In 1872 he published this record in book form and called it *The Underground Railroad*. In the foreword to his book he said: "While I knew the danger of keeping strict records, and while I did not then dream that in my day slavery would be blotted out, or that the time would come when I could publish these records, it used to afford me great satisfaction to take them down, fresh from the lips of fugitives on the way to freedom, and to preserve them as they had given them."

William Still, who was familiar with all the station stops on the Underground Railroad, supplied Harriet with money and sent her and her eleven fugitives on to Burlington, New Jersey.

Harriet felt safer now, though there were danger spots ahead. But the biggest part of her job was over. As they went farther and farther north, it grew colder; she was aware of the wind on the Jersey ferry and aware of the cold damp in New York. From New York they went on to Syracuse, where the temperature was even lower.

In Syracuse she met the Reverend J. W. Loguen, known as "Jarm" Loguen. This was the beginning of a lifelong friendship. Both Harriet and Jarm Loguen were to become friends and supporters of Old John Brown.

From Syracuse they went north again, into a colder, snowier city—Rochester. Here they almost certainly stayed with Frederick Douglass, for he wrote in his autobiography:

"On one occasion I had eleven fugitives at the same time under my roof, and it was necessary for them to remain with me until I could collect sufficient money to get them to Canada. It was the largest number I ever had at any one time, and I had some difficulty in providing so many with food and shelter, but, as may well be imagined, they were not very fastidious in either direction, and were well content with very plain food, and a strip of carpet on the floor for a bed, or a place on the straw in the barnloft."

Late in December, 1851, Harriet arrived in St. Catharines, Canada West (now Ontario), with the eleven fugitives. It had taken almost a month to complete this journey; most of the time had been spent getting out of Maryland.

That first winter in St. Catharines was a terrible one. Canada was a strange frozen land, snow everywhere, ice everywhere, and a bone-biting cold the like of which none of them had ever experienced before. Harriet rented a small frame house in the town and set to work to make a home. The fugitives boarded with her. They worked in the forests, felling trees, and so did she. Sometimes she took other jobs, cooking or cleaning house for people in the town. She cheered on these newly arrived fugitives, working herself, finding work for them, finding food for them, praying for them, sometimes begging for them.

Often she found herself thinking of the beauty of Maryland, the mellowness of the soil, the richness of the plant life there. The climate itself made for an ease of living that could never be duplicated in this bleak, barren countryside.

In spite of the severe cold, the hard work, she came to love St. Catharines, and the other towns and cities in Canada where black men lived. She discovered that freedom meant more than the right to change jobs at will, more than the right to keep the money that one earned. It was the right to vote and to sit on juries. It was the right to be elected to office. In Canada there were black men who were county officials and members of school boards. St. Catharines had a large colony of ex-slaves, and they owned their own homes, kept them neat and clean and in good repair. They lived in whatever part of town they chose and sent their children to the schools.

When spring came she decided that she would make this small Canadian city her home—as much as any place could be said to be home to a woman who traveled from Canada to the Eastern Shore of Maryland as often as she did.

In the spring of 1852, she went back to Cape May, New Jersey. She spent the summer there, cooking in a hotel. That fall she returned, as usual, to Dorchester County, and brought out nine more slaves, conducting them all the way to St. Catharines, in Canada West, to the bone-biting cold, the snow-covered forests—and freedom.

She continued to live in this fashion, spending

the winter in Canada, and the spring and summer working in Cape May, New Jersey, or in Philadelphia. She made two trips a year into slave territory, one in the fall and another in the spring. She now had a definite crystallized purpose, and in carrying it out, her life fell into a pattern which remained unchanged for the next six years.

In April, 1851, Harriet Beecher Stowe (who once described herself in a letter as "a little bit of a woman—somewhat more than forty, about as thin and dry as a pinch of snuff: never very much to look at in my best days, and looking like a used-up article now") sent the first chapter of what she thought would be a short novel to the National Era, *an antislavery weekly published in Washington, D. C. It turned out to be a very long book. Eleven months elapsed before she finished it.*

The book, Uncle Tom's Cabin, or Life Among the Lowly, *was published in two volumes in March, 1852. It was an instantaneous success. Three hundred thousand copies were sold in the first year after its publication. Men and women read it, talked about it, cried over the death of Little Eva and of Uncle Tom, shuddered at the cruelty of Simon Legree. Its influence was incalculable. Many of its readers became foes of the whole system of slavery.*

Before the Civil War, eight different plays based on the life of Uncle Tom had been written and produced, without Mrs. Stowe's consent. During the summer of 1853, Professor Calvin Stowe, Mrs. Stowe's husband, wrote: "The drama of Uncle Tom

"Go On or Die"

has been going on in the National Theatre of New York all summer with most unparalleled success. Everybody goes night after night, and nothing can stop it."

16. "Be Ready to Step On Board"

IN THE FALL of 1854, Harriet Tubman began to feel uneasy about three of her brothers. Benjamin, John and William Henry were still in Maryland, working on plantations where they had been hired out. She kept having dreams about them, vivid dreams in which she saw them sold and sent away in a chain gang. She decided to tell them that she was coming to Maryland that fall, so that they would be ready to go North with her.

It would not be safe to communicate with them directly. She could not read or write. So she had a friend write a cryptic letter to a free Negro, Jacob Jackson, who lived near the plantation where two of her brothers worked.

Jacob had an adopted son who had gone North to live. Harriet thought that it would be perfectly natural and understandable if this son should write to his foster father, reporting about his health and inquiring about the family. She either did not know or had forgotten that the son, William Henry, had no brothers and no "old folks." But Jacob would know what she meant, for he had often provided shelter for her when she was in Dorchester County.

When the letter arrived in Bucktown, the post-master opened it and read it. There was always the possibility that mail with a Northern postmark might contain Abolitionist propaganda, and when it was addressed to a free Negro, it was almost certain to contain objectionable material.

This is what he found: "Read my letter to the old folks, and give my love to them, and tell my brothers to be always *watching unto prayer,* and *when the good old ship of Zion comes along, to be ready to step on board.*" Signed—William Henry Jackson.

The postmaster showed the letter to two other men. They agreed that it must mean something—but the meaning eluded them. They knew that William Henry Jackson had no brothers or sisters. He was an orphan. As for "old folks"—well he didn't have any.

They sent for Jacob, showed him the letter, and asked him for an explanation.

Jacob read the letter quickly, though he pretended to read it slowly, stumbling over the words, repeating some of them, using his finger as a guide, back and forth across the sheet of paper. He wondered how Moses had known that her brothers were in trouble. It was common talk in the cabins that they had been sold and were to go South with the chain gang the day after Christmas. She would get here just in time to rescue them.

He handed the paper with its seemingly meaningless words back to the postmaster. "That letter can't be meant for me nohow," he said, shaking his head. "I can't make head or tail of it."

That same night, Jacob told all three of the Ross

brothers that Moses would be coming for them soon, and to be ready to leave. Benjamin and John worked for Eliza Ann Brodins in Bucktown, William Henry worked on a plantation farther away. They said they would be ready when she came. John said he would be ready, too, but he looked worried.

Harriet made her way South, slowly, without incident. She reached Bucktown on the 23rd of December. The next night she started North again, with a larger party than she had planned for, though John Ross was not with them. Benjamin and William Henry were there. William Henry had brought his fiancée with him, Catherine (or Jane) Kane, a pretty girl, who had been a house servant. She was dressed in a boy's suit, and she looked like an attractive young boy. Then there were two strangers from Cambridge, Peter Jackson and John Chase.

When they were ready to start, John Ross, the third brother, had not arrived. Harriet started without him. She never waited for anyone. Delays were dangerous. She left word with Jacob for him, so that if he did come, he could overtake them along the way. The first stop would be in Caroline County, near Ben's cabin. Old Rit and Ben were now living forty miles to the north of Bucktown, in another county, but on a farm that belonged to Dr. Thompson.

John Ross did overtake them, finally. It was daybreak of Christmas morning when he found them. They were concealed in the fodder house, not far away from the cabin where Old Rit and Ben now lived.

John told them why he was late. His wife had just had another baby. He had to go get the midwife. Then after the baby was born, he couldn't bear to leave her. Yet he knew if he didn't run away, go then, he would be separated from her anyway. Because he was to be sold on the day after Christmas. Though she did not know that. He couldn't bring himself to tell her. At least not then.

So he had lingered in the cabin, looking down at his wife and the newborn baby. Then he had edged toward the door, and each time he moved, his wife had said, "Where you goin', John?"

He had told her he was going to see about being hired out on a new job. They all knew that changes in jobs were arranged during the Christmas season. He thought she believed him. He couldn't bear to tell her he was taking off, couldn't bear to tell her that he had been sold. When he left the cabin, he stood outside the door, listening. He heard her crying and so went back inside.

She said, "Oh, John, you're going to leave me. I know it. But wherever you go, John, don't forget me and the children."

Then he had told her that he was leaving. He said that he would send Moses back for her, on her next trip. He had promised. It wouldn't be long—and in the dim light in the fodder house he looked at Moses for approval, for agreement. She nodded her head. So he felt better.

Then the girl, Catherine, saw John staring at her.

She explained, with a toss of her head, that she was wearing a boy's suit because William Henry had bought it for her. It was the only way she had managed to get away so quickly, and with no trouble. William Henry had left the suit inside the garden fence at the Big House. The garden sloped right down to the river.

When she picked up the bundle William Henry had left for her, she just kept walking down through the garden, down to the river. Crouching under the bank, she had put on the boy's suit, bundled up her own clothes and dropped them into the water, stood a moment watching them float out on the tide. She said, shivering, that it was a queer sight to watch your own clothes, skirts and things, in the water like that.

Then she had walked back through the garden, walked past some of the other maids who had been sent to look for her. When the other girls saw her, they giggled. She strolled right past them, past the house, right out through the gate, and she had heard them saying, what a likely looking little boy, wonder where he came from, wouldn't you like to know him better. She had all she could do to keep from laughing out loud.

William Henry had been waiting for her, just off the plantation, on the road. He brought her right along with him. They'd be married when they got to the North—and freedom.

In 1854, men talked of Kansas and Nebraska, and of the Little Giant—Stephen Douglas, the handsome black-haired Senator from Illinois—who was trying to persuade the Senate to repeal the slavery restriction clause in the Missouri Compromise, as part of his Kansas-Nebraska Bill.

On March 2nd, the Senate passed the Kansas-Nebraska Bill which repealed the Missouri Compromise restriction and divided the Nebraska Territory into two territories: Kansas and Nebraska. In May President Pierce signed the Bill.

And it was in May that the most dramatic of the fugitive slave cases began to unfold in Boston. Anthony Burns, a fugitive slave, who had escaped from his master in Virginia, was arrested and held in the Boston Courthouse. After a three-day trial, the United States Commissioner, Edward G. Loring, decided that Burns must be returned to his master. On June 2nd he was escorted to the Long Wharf in Boston and put aboard a revenue cutter and sent back to Virginia.

The temper of Boston had changed. The biggest factor in that change was the Kansas-Nebraska Bill, for men in the North felt that the South had gone back on its promises, that its intention was to extend slavery all over the United States.

On the 2nd of June, 1854, when Anthony Burns walked toward the Long Wharf through streets lined with marines and cavalry, guarded by one thousand policemen, bells were tolled. The houses and the shops were draped in black. As the procession which surrounded Burns moved down toward the wharf, it was met with a perfect howl of "Shame! Shame!" and hisses.

In the North, men said that it had cost anywhere between forty and a hundred thousand dollars for the United States Government to return Burns to his master. They said it showed how powerful the slaveholding South had become, that part of the United States Army should have been called out to assure the return of one miserable fugitive. More important, they said they would work to make the Fugitive Slave Law a joke, make it as worthless as the Compromise of 1820, which the South had agreed to and then junked as part of the Kansas-Nebraska Bill.

In the South, members of the slaveholding class were disturbed. With the opening of vast new territories, slaves had tripled in value. The South held more than 3,000,000 slaves, estimated to be worth one billion dollars. If the temper of a city like Boston had changed so that it was necessary to call forth a small army to assure the safe return of one fugitive, then it boded ill for the future. It suggested that one billion dollars' worth of the South's property was insecure.

17. "Moses Arrives with Six Passengers"

HARRIET TUBMAN had experienced moments of envy when she listened to the story that John Ross had told, heard the warmth in Catherine's voice when she spoke William Henry's name.

After they finished talking, she frowned, forcing herself to think of something other than John Tubman, and marriages and children, and engagements and the tenderness in a man's voice when he spoke of his wife.

It was still raining. From the dark, heavy look of the sky, visible through the roof of the fodder house, it would be an all-day rain. Christmas Day. And a Sunday. The beat of the rain against the roof of the fodder house, against its sides, would be their only Christmas greeting. She hoped they wouldn't resent it too much.

There were wide chinks in the walls. Through them she could see the sway-backed cabin where Daddy Ben and Old Rit lived. It looked exactly like the cabin on the Brodas plantation where she was born. A whole row of these sway-backed cabins here, too. Smoke kept pouring out of the clay-daubed chimney, hanging heavy in the air. Old Rit had probably killed her pig, and was cooking it for the Christmas dinner. The master gave her a baby pig every year, and she fattened it, saving food from her own plate to feed the pig, so that she could feed her family with a lavish hand on this one day. She'd have pork and sausage and bacon. Plenty of food. The boys said that Old Rit was expecting them for dinner. They always spent Christmas Day with her.

She had to figure out some way of letting Ben know that she was here, that the boys were with her and that they needed food. It would never do to let Old Rit know this. She would laugh and shout. Then when she learned, as she certainly would, that the boys were running away, going North, she would try to detain them, would create such an uproar that the entire quarter would know their secret.

Harriet remembered the two men, John Chase and Peter Jackson. They were strangers. She asked them to go to the cabin, to tell Ben that his children were in the fodder house, badly in need of food. She warned them not to let Old Rit overhear what they said.

John and Peter did exactly as she told them. She watched them knock on the ramshackle door of the cabin, saw the door open, saw Old Ben standing in the doorway. The men motioned to him to come outside. They talked to him. Ben nodded his head. His expression did not change at all. She thought, how wonderful he is. Then he went back inside the cabin.

Late in the afternoon, he tapped on the side of the fodder house, and then opened the door, and put part of the Christmas dinner—cooked bacon, hoecake, fried pork and roasted yams—inside on the floor. He did not look at them. He said, "I know what'll come of this and I ain't goin' *to see my children,* nohow."

Harriet remembered his reputation for truthfulness. His word had always been accepted on the plantation because he was never known to tell a lie. She felt a kind of wondering admiration for him. He had become an old man in the five years since she had seen him—an old man. Yet the integrity and the strength of his character had not changed. How badly he must have wanted to see them, four of his children, there in the fodder house, on Christmas Day; but he would not lie, and so he would not look at them. Thus, if he was questioned as to the whereabouts of his boys, he could say that he had not seen them.

He made three trips from the cabin to the fodder house. Each time he put a small bundle of food inside the door until he must have given them most of the food intended for the Christmas dinner. Harriet noticed how slow his movements were. He was stooped over. He had aged fast. She would have to come back soon for him and Old Rit. Some time very soon. She remembered his great strength, and his love for his broadax, and the stories he used to tell her about the wonderful things to be seen in the woods. She wanted to put her arms around him and look deep into his eyes and didn't because she respected his right to make this self-sacrificing contribution to their safety. How he must have wanted to look at them, especially at the daughter whom he had not seen for five long years.

They stayed in the fodder house all that day, lying on top of the corn, listening to the drip of the rain, waiting for dark, when they would set out. They spoke in whispers.

Harriet kept reassuring them. They were perfectly safe. They would not be missed for at least two days. At Christmas everyone was busy, dancing, laughing. The masters were entertaining their friends and relatives in their big, comfortable houses. The slaves were not required to work—as long as the Yule logs burned in the fireplaces. She had never lost a passenger, never run her train off the track, they were safe with her, the Lord would see them through.

She knew they did not like this long rainy day spent inside a fodder house, rain coming through the chinks in the boards. Dainty, pretty Catherine, who had been a house servant, complained bitterly. She objected to the rough feel of the corn. She said she thought she heard the sound of rats, a dry scrabbling sound.

Harriet laughed at her, and told her this was easy, just sitting around like this, that the Underground Railroad wasn't any train ride. It meant walking, and sometimes running, and being hungry, and sometimes jouncing up and down in the bottom of a farmer's wagon, but more walking than riding, rain or dry, through woods and swamps and briars and hiding anywhere that the earth offered a little shelter against prying eyes and listening ears.

It meant not enough sleep because the walking had to be done at night and the sleeping during the day. Before the journey ended, Catherine would be able to sleep anywhere, on the ground, in a haystack, under a bush, and this rat-infested fodder house would loom in her memory like a king's palace.

Catherine let out a scream and then burst into tears and William Henry put his arm around her to comfort her. Harriet could not look at them. She turned her back on them, thinking not for her, ever, that soft light in a man's eyes.

She looked through one of the chinks in the wall, looked toward the cabin. Every few minutes Old Rit came to the door, opened it, and looked out, hand shading her eyes, frowning, peering toward the road. Harriet thought, She's looking for the boys, wondering why William Henry and John and Benjamin haven't come, wondering what could have happened to them. The possibilities were infinite. They might have been sold South. They might have run away and been caught, might now be in chains. They might have kept going and been shot out-of-hand.

Late in the afternoon, Ben made one more trip. He pushed another bundle of food inside the door. He kept his eyes closed, tight shut. He said he would be back when it got dark and would walk with them just a little way, to visit with them.

At dusk Harriet left the fodder house. She moved quietly toward the cabin. She wanted to get a good look at her mother. The door was ajar. Old Rit was sitting in front of the fireplace, her head on her

147

hand. The flickering light from the fire played over her. Harriet saw a little old woman, rocking her body back and forth, sitting on her heels, in front of the fire, sucking on a clay pipe as she grieved about her boys.

Harriet wanted to say something to her, to offer some word of comfort, of greeting, and dared not for fear Old Rit's uncontrolled joy or her loudly expressed fears would attract attention.

When night came, Ben tapped at the door. He had tied a bandanna tight around his eyes. Harriet took one of his arms and one of the boys took him by the other arm. They started out, walking slowly.

Harriet answered Ben's questions as fast as she could, she told him a little about the other trips she had made, said that she would be back again to get him and Old Rit, told him where some of the people were that she had piloted North, what the North was like, cold in winter, yes, but there were worse things in the world than cold. She told him about St. Catharines, in Canada, and said that she would be back—soon.

They parted from him reluctantly. Ben stood in the middle of the road, listening to the sound of their footsteps. They kept looking back at him. He did not remove the blindfold until he was certain they were out of sight. When he could hear no sound of movement, he untied the bandanna and went back to the cabin.

The next day, Monday, the brothers should have been back on the plantations where they worked. By afternoon, their temporary masters, disturbed by their absence, sent messengers to Dr. Thompson, in Caroline County, asking about them. Dr. Thompson said, "Why, they generally come to see the house servants when they come home for Christmas, but this time they haven't been round at all. Better go down to Old Ben's and ask him."

They questioned Old Rit first. She said, "Not one of 'em came this Christmas. I was looking for 'em all day, and my heart's most broke about 'em not coming."

Ben said, "I haven't *seen* one of 'em this Christmas."

Meanwhile Harriet led her group through the woods. Sometimes she ventured on the road and they stumbled along behind her over the frozen ruts. Sometimes she took them through fields, sodden, gray. As they moved slowly North, through Camden, Dover, Smyrna, Blackbird, she became aware of the heavy brooding silence that hung over them. She told them about Thomas Garrett, and the food and the warmth of the welcome that awaited them in Wilmington, and thought of the many different times she had invoked the image of the tall, powerfully built Quaker with the kind eyes, to reassure herself, as well as a group of runaways who stumbled along behind her.

They stopped at a house in Middletown and spent the night and part of the day. Then they continued their journey, on through New Castle, down the New Castle Road, until they reached the bank of the Christiana River. Across the river, cold and gray in the dusk of a winter's night, lay Wilmington.

Harriet waited until it was dark and then she herded her party along, over the bridge, and then straight toward Thomas Garrett's house. Garrett fed them and hastily sent them on their way to Philadelphia that same night. The next day Garrett wrote a letter to J. Miller McKim, to let him know that this party of fugitives was on its way:

Wilmington, 12 mo. 29th, 1854

Esteemed Friend, J. Miller McKim:—

We made arrangements last night, and sent away Harriet Tubman, with six men and one woman to Allen Agnew's, to be forwarded across the country to the city. Harriet, and one of the men, had worn their shoes off their feet, and I gave them two dollars to help fit them out, and directed a carriage to be hired at my expense, to take them out, but do not yet know the expense. I now have two more from the lowest county in Maryland, on the Peninsula, upwards of one hundred miles. I will try to get one of our trusty colored men to take them to-morrow morning to the Anti-Slavery office. You can pass them on.

THOMAS GARRETT

They arrived safely at the office of the Philadelphia Vigilance Committee on the 29th of December, late at night. William Still wrote their names down in his record book under the heading

"Moses Arrives With Six Passengers." He described Harriet as "a woman of no pretensions, indeed, a more ordinary specimen of humanity could hardly be found among the most unfortunate-looking farm hands of the South. . . .

"Her success was wonderful. Time and again she made successful visits to Maryland on the Underground Rail Road, and would be absent for weeks at a time, running daily risks while making preparations for herself and passengers. Great fears were entertained for her safety, but she seemed wholly devoid of personal fear. The idea of being captured by slave-hunters or slave-holders, seemed never to enter her mind."

He mentioned the sleeping seizures. "Half of her time, she had the appearance of one asleep, and would actually sit down by the road-side and go fast asleep when on her errands of mercy through the South. . . ."

Before he described the passengers she had brought, he offered a theory as to the reason for her successful trips. "It is obvious enough, however, that her success in going into Maryland as she did, was attributable to her adventurous spirit and utter disregard of consequences. Her like it is probable was never known before or since."

As to the passengers, John Chase was twenty years old, "chestnut color, of spare build and smart." He said that his master, John Campbell Henry, of Cambridge, Maryland, was a "hard man and that he owned about one hundred and forty slaves." Benjamin Ross was described as "twenty-eight years of age, chestnut color, medium size and shrewd." John Ross was "only twenty-two and had left his wife Harriet Ann . . . and two small children." "Peter Jackson had been hired out to a farmer near Cambridge." Catherine (or Jane) was twenty-two and said her master "was the worst man in the country." William Henry Ross was "thirty-five years of age, of a chestnut color, and well made," and said that he had "hardly been treated as well as a gentleman would treat a dumb brute."

William Still gave them advice "on the subject of temperance, industry, education, etc. Clothing, food and money were also given them to meet their wants, and they were sent on their way rejoicing."

After they left Philadelphia, they were guided to New York City, and then on up through New York state, stopping at various stations on the underground route in Albany, in Utica. They stayed with Reverend J. W. Loguen in Syracuse, and with Frederick Douglass in Rochester.

As they went farther and farther west it grew colder. But the icy wind and the snow were only a prelude to the low temperatures they found in Canada. They arrived in St. Catharines, Canada West, early in January of 1855.

Day after day, Harriet listened as all six of them complained bitterly about the cold that stung their faces, numbed their fingers, frosted their feet. Finally, one night when they were sitting huddled around the fire in the small house where she lived, she became impatient.

"It's warm in Maryland, nice and warm down

there in the Tidewater country, compared to here," she said. "You want to go back there?"

They were startled into silence. She knew they were weighing this new freedom in the balance. Was it better to be warm and be a slave? Or was it better to be cold and to be free? Then they said, No, in unison. Even Catherine, the delicately pretty girl who had been a house servant, said, No, she did not want to go back though she was shivering from the cold.

Harriet poked the fire. "It would have surprised me if you'd said, Yes. I've seen hundreds and hundreds of slaves who finally got to the North and freedom. But I never yet saw one who was willing to go back South and be a slave."

She thought, Freedom's a hard-bought thing, not bought with dust, but bought with all of oneself —the bones, the spirit and the flesh—and once obtained it had to be cherished, no matter what the cost.

She would help these six people get adjusted to life in St. Catharines, and then in a few more months she would go back to Maryland to help another group of slaves escape. Nothing would ever stop her from helping them, not masters or slave catchers, or overseers or fugitive slave laws.

"If being cold is part of the price of being free then we'll just have to pay it," she said, and sat up even straighter. "We got to go free—or die."

Late in the summer of 1855, John Brown arrived in Kansas with a wagonload of arms and ammuni-

tion. Four of his sons had taken up land there in October, 1854. It was obvious from the letters he had received from them that the "Kansas troubles" would have to be settled with guns.

Brown was fifty-six years old. His hair was gray. His shoulders were stooped. Men already spoke of him as Old Brown.

18. A Wagon Load of Bricks

FROM 1851 to 1857, the country moved closer to civil war. During these years Harriet Tubman made eleven trips into Maryland to bring out slaves.

In November, 1856, she rescued Joe Bailey. In the spring she had made two trips to the Eastern Shore. The result of one of these trips is recorded in Still's *Underground Railroad:* "April 1856. The next arrival numbered four passengers, and came under the guidance of 'Moses' (Harriet Tubman) from Maryland. . . ."

The second trip, which took place in May, is mentioned in a letter that Thomas Garrett wrote to J. Miller McKim and William Still of the Philadelphia Vigilance Committee:

> Wilmington, 5 mo. 11th, 1856
> Esteemed Friends—McKim and Still:—
> . . . . Those four I wrote thee about arrived safe up in the neighborhood of Longwood, and Harriet Tubman followed after in the stage yesterday. I shall expect five more from the same neighborhood next trip. . . .
>
> As ever your friend,
> THOS. GARRETT

The November trip started off inauspiciously. There were three men in the group: Joe Bailey and his brother William, and a man named Peter Pennington. There was one woman, Eliza Nokey.

After Harriet heard Joe's story, her fear of immediate pursuit increased. Joe was a tall, dark man, muscular and handsome. His master had hired him out to another planter, William R. Hughlett, for six years. Finally, Hughlett decided to buy him, for Joe supervised the running of the plantation so well that Hughlett didn't have to pay an overseer. He paid two thousand dollars for Joe.

Joe said the day Hughlett bought him, he beat him with a rawhide, to make certain Joe knew who was the master. Joe told them that he had said to himself, "This is the first and the last time." That night he took a boat and rowed down the river to the plantation where Old Ben lived. He told Ben, "The next time Moses comes, let me know."

The scars on Joe's back weren't healed yet. Harriet worried about that. His height, the bloody stripes on his back, would make it easy to identify him. Perhaps it was the worry, the haste with which they had to move to get away, the fact she felt impelled to urge them to move faster and faster; anyway, her head began to ache. She made them walk along the edge of the road, dangerous, but going through the woods was too slow. As she hurried them along, the scar from the old wound on her temple began to throb like a toothache. The ache in her head increased. She could feel sleep creeping over her like a paralysis. She tried to sing, tried to fight off the sleep, and stumbled, went down on her knees. And was sound asleep.

When she awakened, she had no idea how long she had slept. She heard a man's voice saying, "You've got to trust her. When she has those sleeps you have to leave her alone till she wakes up, she'll wake up pretty soon."

It was Joe who had spoken. He was squatting on his heels, and Eliza and Bill and Peter were standing up, looking down at her. She was lying flat on the road. The sun was shining, sunlight so brilliant that she thought she could feel it warm on her eyelids. Yet the ground was cold, the air was cold.

She got to her feet quickly. Her heart seemed to be skipping beats; it was going so fast. They were out in plain sight, all of them; anyone who passed would recognize them for what they were—runaways, fugitives.

She ordered them to follow her and went into the woods that bordered the road, plunging into the woods, almost running. They came behind her, and it seemed to her their footsteps kept pace with the speed of her thoughts: should have been traveling at night, not in broad daylight; should have been concealed, not out in the open like that; got to go faster and faster, faster, faster.

Then she heard them muttering. One of the men said, "She's taking us back, I can tell, we're going back the same way we come, the woman's crazy—"

She led them on a zigzag course, up a hill and then down. At the foot of the hill there was a small river which followed a winding course. She went straight toward it.

Eliza Nokey said, panic in her voice, "You goin' wade that?"

Harriet said she had had a dream while she was sleeping. And in the dream she had seen this river.

Eliza said it was too deep to wade, they'd all drown.

Harriet said she was certain there was one place so shallow that they could wade it.

They stopped following her. All of them stopped. Bill asked her if she'd crossed this river before. She said no, but she'd seen it in her dream, that the Lord told her what to do, and running water leaves no trail. They would be safe on the other side.

Peter Pennington said, "I'll wade no freezin' water for no crazy woman," and started back toward the woods.

She raised the gun, pointed it, scowling. "Stand still," she ordered. "You try to go back, try to run back to the woods, and you'll never run any more. You go on with me or you die."

They went on. She didn't like it, the threat of violence always disturbed her. And she had never felt so unsure of herself, so desperate, so afraid. But her visions had never failed her.

She waded into the stream, water like ice was around her ankles, and as she went forward, it reached her thighs, and then her waist. She turned and looked back, and Joe was the only one who had followed her. The others were standing on the bank watching. Water reached to her shoulders and she kept going. She closed her eyes for a moment, in the grip of a despair as icy cold as the water.

She thought that if her belief were only strong enough, the waters of this stream would have parted, and they would all have walked across on dry land; instead the water rose higher, now it was above her shoulders, up to her chin. She kept going. She held the gun up out of the water; at least Joe was still following; and she thought, Wade in the water just like John, and a feeling of confidence returned. When the Lord no longer wanted her—

The water began to recede. It was down to her shoulders. But it wasn't the water that was receding, the stream was getting shallower. When the others saw this, they started to wade the river, too. Then all of them reached the opposite bank, dry land, a small island, or neck of land. They were shivering, shocked by the cold, numb, but otherwise unharmed.

They went through more woods and then they came to a clearing. There was a cabin there. Harriet said she had seen that in her dreams, too. They would be safe there.

And they were. The cabin belonged to a family of free Negroes. They were made welcome, given food. Their wet clothing was dried in front of the open fire.

The next morning they set out again. They went back the same way they had come, but they did not have to wade through the river. Their host served as guide, and he led them by a long roundabout road.

When they reached the spot where Harriet had gone to sleep by the side of the road, the day before, they all shivered. The patrollers had been there, had waited for them there. If they hadn't crossed that river at Harriet's direction, they would have been caught. The evidence was unmistakable: the grass had been trampled by horses' feet; the ground was littered with the stubs of half-smoked cigars.

A poster had been nailed to one of the trees. They recognized it immediately. In the upper left-hand corner there was a woodcut of a black man, a small running figure with a stick over his shoulder, and a bundle tied to the end of the stick, and another stick in his hand.

Harriet tore the poster down, and handed it to Joe. He read it aloud:

HEAVY REWARD

TWO THOUSAND SIX HUNDRED DOLLARS REWARD.—Ran away from the subscriber, on Saturday night, November 15th, 1856, Josiah and William Bailey, and Peter Pennington. Joe is about 5 feet 10 inches in height, of a chestnut color, bald head, with a remarkable scar on one of his cheeks, not positive on which it is, but think it is on the left, under the eye, has intelligent countenance, active, and well-made. He is about 28 years old. Bill is of a darker color, about 5 feet 8 inches in height, stammers a little when confused, well-made, and older than Joe, well dressed, but may have pulled kearsey on over their other clothes. Peter is smaller than either the others, about 25 years of age, dark chestnut color, 5 feet 7 or 8 inches high.

A reward of fifteen hundred dollars will be given to any person who will apprehend the said Joe Bailey, and lodge him safely in the jail at Easton, Talbot Co., Md. and $300 for Bill and $800 for Peter.

W. R. HUGHLETT,
John C. Henry,
T. WRIGHT

When Joe finished reading, there was silence. Harriet tried to say something, and her voice was only a croaking sound in her throat. Again she tried to speak, and couldn't. She must have caught cold from the river. What would she do? Bill sighed. Then Peter groaned.

Eliza Nokey was angry. No one had offered any reward for her return. Then Joe started to sing. He looked at that poster which meant any man who read it would be tempted to start hunting for the slave who was worth fifteen hundred dollars to his master, crumpled it up in his hand, and started to sing.

They hurried in a northerly direction, and Joe kept singing, softly, under his breath:

The little wheel run by faith,
  And the big wheel run by the grace of
    God:
A wheel within a wheel
  Way in the middle of the air.

As they went along, Harriet sensed danger everywhere, smelled danger. They were not safe. She herded them along, sometimes going ahead of them, sometimes walking behind them, prodding them with the butt of the gun. The hoarseness prevented her from speaking.

It was Joe who talked, Joe who encouraged them, Joe who, as if by instinct, told the old stories about the slave ships, the torture, the irons and the whips. When he sang, they moved faster. Eliza Nokey fairly skipped along, as Joe sang, his voice almost a whisper:

Who comes yonder all dressed in red?
I heard the angels singing—
It's all the children Moses led,
I heard the angels singing.

They saw other places along the road where the patrollers had been, found one place where they must have waited for as much as an hour, in the hope that they would be able to find some trace of this party. The horses had been tied to the trees.

Joe shook his head and stopped singing.

It was daybreak when they reached the outskirts of Wilmington. Within sight of the long bridge Harriet called a halt. She told the runaways to hide in the woods, not to speak to anyone, not to make a sound, not to move.

She watched the bridge for a long time. It was guarded. There were posters nailed to the trees all along the road. Stealthily, cautiously, she took two of the posters down, and went back to where she'd left the runaways. Joe said one of the posters was the one he'd read to them before and the reward for him had been increased to two thousand dollars.

But the other—the little running figure reproduced on the flimsy paper—was that of a woman. The reward offered for her capture was twelve thousand dollars. The poster described her. It said she was dark, short, of a muscular build, with a deep voice, and that she had a scar on her left temple, scars on the back of her neck. Her name was Harriet Tubman. Sometimes she was called Moses.

Harriet laughed. She said nobody was going to catch her. She left them again and went as close to the bridge as she dared, waiting, watching. Thomas Garrett must know about those posters, must know the bridge was watched. He would try to get in touch with her. She was certain of it.

He did. Garrett sent his servant out to look for Harriet. When Harriet saw him, she signaled to him. They held a conference in the long grass by the side of the road. Then he went back to report to Garrett. Two hours later he was back again with Garrett's message.

It was dark when Harriet returned to the fugitives. As she went toward their hiding place, she signaled her approach by singing:

"Go down, Moses—"

Her voice was no longer beautiful. It was like the croaking of a frog, hoarse, tuneless.

She told them to follow her. She took them through the woods, and then along a road, heavy woods on each side of it, more like a country lane than a road. There was a long wagon there. And men. And the sound of horses, jingle of harness, stamping of feet, soft blowing out of breath.

They got in the wagon, one by one, and lay down flat. Harriet said the men were bricklayers. She said that the men would cover them with bricks. When the men put boards over them, Eliza Nokey made a thin high sound of terror, and Harriet heard her whisper, "It's like being in a coffin." Then the bricks were placed on top of the boards. Harriet thought, Eliza is right—it is as though we had died together and been buried in a common grave, and croaked, "We got to go free or die." The words were lost.

The wagon started. There was a sound of hoofbeats. The men on the wagon began to laugh and shout and sing. Then they were on the long bridge and someone cried, "Halt!"

The driver shouted, "Whoa! Whoa!"

When he was asked if he'd seen any runaway Negroes, he laughed and said with that kind of money being offered for them, he planned to start hunting for them as soon as he got home, right after supper.

When they got out of the wagon at Thomas Garrett's house in Wilmington, Garrett said of Harriet, "She was so hoarse she could hardly speak, and was also suffering with violent toothache."

Garrett forwarded them to Philadelphia where William Still wrote down their past history in his record book. From Philadelphia they were forwarded to the office of the Antislavery Society in New York.

When they reached New York, it was Joe who lost his courage. The moment they entered the office of Oliver Johnson, head of the New York Antislavery Society, Johnson glanced at Joe and said, "Well, Joe, I'm glad to see the man who is worth two thousand dollars to his master."

Joe looked as though he were going to faint. He said, "How did you know me, sir?"

"Here is the advertisement. From the description, no one could possibly mistake you."

"How far off is Canada?" Joe asked.

Oliver Johnson showed him a map. "It's more than three hundred miles, by railroad."

Joe said he wouldn't go any farther because he would be hunted every step of the way, and he couldn't stand it any longer. If a man who had never seen him could recognize him from the description, then the whole dream of freedom was hopeless. He told Harriet to take the others and go on. None of them would be safe as long as he was with them.

But Harriet said they would not go without him. Finally, reluctantly, he went with them. She said afterward, "From that time Joe was silent. He talked no more. He sang no more. He sat with his head on his hand, and nobody could rouse him, or make him take any interest in anything."

They were put aboard a train and they passed through New York state without incident. The conductor had hidden them in the baggage car, but when they approached Niagara Falls, he took them into one of the coaches.

Harriet tried to rouse Joe from his apathy, and urged him to look at Niagara. But he still sat with his head in his hands, refusing to look.

Then she shouted, "You've crossed the line! You're free, Joe, you're free!"

The others shouted too. Still he sat, bent over, silent. Harriet shook him. "Joe! Joe! You're a free man!"

Slowly he straightened up in his seat, and then stood up, and lifted his hands, and began to sing. There were tears streaming down his cheeks as he sang, louder and louder:

> *Glory to God and Jesus, too,*
> *One more soul got safe.*
> *Glory to God and Jesus, too,*
> *For all these souls got safe.*

His voice was like the sound of thunder. Harriet, listening, thought it put a glory over all of them.

By 1856 there was civil war in Kansas. In April, May and June, most of the speeches made in Congress concerned Kansas.

Toward the end of May, Old John Brown, accompanied by four of his sons, a son-in-law and two other men, headed for Pottawatomie, where they murdered five pro-slavery settlers, an action which set off guerrilla warfare- in Kansas. Henceforth John Brown was known as Bloody Brown or Pottawatomie Brown.

19. The Old Folks Go North

IN JUNE OF 1857, Harriet was again working in a hotel in Cape May, New Jersey. While she was there she kept having vivid dreams about Old Rit and Ben, her mother and father. In the dream they were about to be sold. Off and on during the day she would shiver, remembering the sad expression on Old Rit's face.

She had always wanted to bring them North. But she did not know how she could travel with two old people. All her other passengers, with the exception of the babies, had been young and strong, able to walk long distances. The babies were no problem, light as air to carry. Sometimes she carried them herself in a basket, and she always gave them a few drops of paregoric so they would keep quiet. A group of runaways could travel just as fast with a baby as without one. But Old Rit and Ben—

It was with a shrug of her shoulders that she started South to get them, thinking that she'd solved all kinds of problems and, with the help of the good Lord, she'd solve this one when she got there. There was an urgency about the dreams that suggested she could waste no time.

She went South by train, counting on the fact that no one would question her because she was going in the wrong direction for a runaway slave. It was broad daylight when she reached Bucktown, Maryland. She deliberately assumed the bent-over posture of an old woman, sidling down the street. She pulled her sunbonnet well over her eyes. There was always the chance she might be recognized because she had lived and worked in and around this area.

She stopped once, at a cabin where a family of free Negroes lived. She bought a pair of fowl from them, and asked that their legs be tied together. As she paid for the chickens she thought it takes a lot of cooking and cleaning and scrubbing to pay for these trips but it's worth it.

When she left Bucktown the chickens were fluttering and squawking and she looked for all the world like an old woman. She was not disguised; it was simply that the bent back and the chickens, legs tied together, transformed her into a granny, obviously coming from or going to market. The chickens would serve to distract the attention of anyone who passed her.

She walked along the dirt road, thinking about Barrett's slave, and how he had run down this same road, with the overseer close behind him, and she behind the overseer. She touched the deep scar on her forehead, remembering. She had worked in these woods that were so close to the road, swinging an ax just like a man. Sometimes she had walked here with John Tubman. She knew a moment of self-pity, of regret, thinking of the quilt she had made, reliving all the tender dreams that had gone into the making of it. She sighed. It had, in all truth, been freedom's quilt. It was the only gift she had to give to the woman who had helped set her feet firmly on the road to freedom.

Far down the road she heard the pound, pound, pound of horses' hoofs. She stood still, undecided. Should she hide in the woods? She gathered up her long skirt in one hand, preparing to run. She wouldn't run. Her skirt would be snagged and torn by briars, she might trip and fall. Besides, she still did not know how she was going to get Old Rit and Ben to the North. She might have to take them on a train, and she couldn't ride on a train with her clothing torn, it was one of the earmarks of the fugitive.

As the hoofbeats grew nearer, she pulled her sunbonnet farther down over her face and shortened the length of her steps, edging over to the side of the narrow road, hitching along. When the horse came abreast of her, she looked up, sidewise, at the rider. It was Doc Thompson, her old master, cigar in his mouth. She caught a glimpse of his heavy gold watch chain, of his broad-brimmed Panama hat.

She gave a hard violent jerk at the string on the chickens' legs, and with a squawk and a wild fluttering of wings, the chickens ran back down the road. Harriet gave a high-pitched, quavering screech and hobbled after them.

Doc Thompson reined in his horse, turned to watch the pursuit. He laughed and then he shouted,

"Go it, Granny! I'll bet on the chickens but go it anyway, Granny! Ha! Ha! Ha!"

She stopped running as soon as she heard him cluck to the horse, and when the hoofbeats started again, she turned and walked purposefully toward the plantation, back straight, head held proudly. She lingered near the edge of the road until it was dark. Then she went toward the quarter, moving so quietly that she was only a shadow that emerged from deeper shadows, disappeared, emerged again. She tapped on the door, lightly.

Slow footsteps approached the door. Old Rit opened the door a little way and said, "Who is it?" caution in her voice.

"It's Hat," Harriet whispered.

She was afraid that Old Rit would exclaim, loudly, laugh and cry, and everyone in the quarter would know that she had come back.

But Old Rit merely said, "Come in. I didn't think I'd ever see you again."

They stood looking at each other for a moment and then Old Rit hugged Harriet and kissed her. Harriet looked at her mother, frowning, wondering how in the world she was going to make the trip North with her. Old Rit moved slowly, stiffly.

"I've got a misery in my knees and my back all the time," she explained, apologetically. "Even on a night like this I keep a little fire going. It kind of helps my legs."

Harriet could see that her mother was troubled by something. She was very glad to see her but she seemed worried.

"Where's Daddy Ben?" she asked.

Old Rit sighed. "He's up to the Big House. They keep asking him questions. They say your daddy helped hide Barrett's Peter. That he put him in the corncrib and fed him. I'd of never let that worth-nothing Peter stay here, and I'd of never took food to him. Food we should have been eating—"

"Well, what happened?" Harriet asked.

"Peter he took off after he stayed here five days. Then he got scared walking through the woods, and he turned around and come back, and told his wife that your daddy helped him. And she went and told her master about your daddy. And now they say he's been running off slaves—"

The door opened and Ben entered the cabin. He stared at Harriet as though he didn't believe she was real. He said, "Hat! You come back for us, didn't you?"

She could only nod. It didn't seem possible that Ben, too, could have grown so much older, so slow, so bent-over. Ben hugged her and patted her arm.

Old Rit said, "What'd they ask you this time?"

"The same thing over and over. 'Did you see Barrett's Peter?'"

"How do you answer them?" Harriet asked curiously.

"I just keep saying I ain't never seen him in the corncrib—and I ain't. It was dark in there and I never did really see him. That first time when I opened the door it was moonrise and he was right close to the door. I had thought there were rats got in there again. I got good ears and I heard a kind of rustle noise. I got a big stick and I went so quiet he never even heard me open the door. The moon shine was right on his face and I could see his eyes." Ben covered his own eyes with his hand for a moment. "Anybody would have fed him," he said, "anybody with a heart. You could tell how scared he was and how long he'd been scared and how long he'd been starving just by his eyes. He told me he'd been in the corncrib for two days without nothing to eat because he left Mr. Barrett's place without taking no food with him. I saw hunger and I saw fear but I didn't see him."

Harriet remembered how Ben had blindfolded himself so he wouldn't "see" her that Christmas night she stayed in the corncrib with a party of fugitives.

Ben went on talking in his old man's voice. "I couldn't bear not to feed him. And then one night I went out there with some hoecake and a bit of fish and he weren't there. I knew he'd took off and two days straight I prayed that he'd make it. Next thing I heard he were back. He told his wife he couldn't stand the lonely dark and the not knowing where he was going so he come back and he told her I helped him. So she told Mr. Barrett and Mr. Barrett told the Master."

Old Rit said drearily, "They keep asking him questions about it. Every time he goes up to the Big House I'm scared he won't come back."

"The Master wouldn't let nothing happen to me," Ben said. "He said I'd been a good slave and he wouldn't let nobody abuse me or arrest me. But he said the others like Mr. Barrett was getting madder and madder at him because they think I got something to do with the man they call—" he hesitated, looked around the cabin, and then whispered the word, "Moses."

Old Rit said, "Hush!"

Harriet said, "Will they ask you about Peter again tomorrow?"

"They been asking me every day for a week now. Of course they'll ask me again tomorrow. Mr. Barrett he comes to the Big House and the Master sends for me and they talk and smoke and argue. And the Master says, 'I got to believe Ben. He ain't never been known to tell a lie, and if Ben belong to you, you'd believe him too. He ain't the one that run away. Peter's the one that run away. Ben ain't the one that run away and then got scared and come back. Whyn't you go ask some of those free Negroes about Peter? Ben's an old man and been on this plantation all his life. He ain't the one's been running off the slaves around here!' "

Harriet thought, I can see them as he tells it, see the cigar smoke and the long cold drinks, see Doc Thompson enjoying Barrett's irritation, smiling through the cigar smoke, toying with his gold watch chain.

Ben said, "Then Mr. Barrett he gets mad and leaves. Jumps on that big white horse and jerks at the reins and goes off, cursing and swearing at the horse, his face all red. And the Master and I know he's really cursing us and not the horse. And then the Master says, 'He'll be back tomorrow, Ben.'"

While Ben was talking, part of Harriet's mind was still trying to figure out how she was going to get these two elderly people away from here. If she could get them to Thomas Garrett in Wilmington, everything would be all right. But how get them there? They simply could not walk. Well, if they couldn't walk, they'd have to ride.

"It'll be all right," she said confidently. "Daddy Ben, let's you and me go outside for a while."

Once outside the cabin she put her hand on his arm. "I've got to have a horse," she said. "You'll have to tell me where I can get one. It's the only way I can get you folks away from here."

"A horse?" He shook his head. "It ain't easy to get hold of one since so many slaves run off." He thought a long time. Finally he said, "There's Dollie Mae. That's that old critter they mostly keep out to pasture over to Mr. Barrett's. But it's a good mile to their plantation."

"A mile?" she said and laughed. "Why, I've walked—" and she stopped. "I'll get the horse. You and Mammy get yourselves ready to leave. Pack up whatever food you've got. I'll be back for you."

She found Dollie Mae lying down under some trees in Barrett's pasture. Someone had left a long rope around her neck. She got the horse up, patted her, talked to her. My, but she's old, she thought. I just hope she'll be able to make the trip.

The stars were out and the air was warm. She got on Dollie's back with difficulty because of the

175

long skirt, and went down the road toward the quarter. True, she had the horse but she needed a wagon and she would need reins of some kind. Well, she'd just have to borrow some things from Doc Thompson. There used to be an old wagon in back of the stable.

She tied the horse to a tree in the woods near the quarter. Then she went behind the stable, moving cautiously. Sure enough, there was the wagon. So far, so good. Next thing was to get inside the stable. Warm night, doors ajar. She pushed them back and they made no sound. Someone evidently kept them greased. Once inside she got the harness and—

She heard a sound behind her, turned. The groom or hostler, a man she had never seen, was standing in the door, eyes wide with fright. They looked at each other in silence, not moving. Then she put her finger to her lips and shook her head, and backed out of the stable as quietly as she had entered it.

Would he give the alarm? She'd just have to risk it. She went back to the tree where she'd left Dollie, harnessed her up, urged her toward the stable, stopping every once in a while to listen. Nothing. She backed Dollie between the shafts of the old wagon, hurrying now.

Once on the seat she clucked softly. The wagon started moving, creaking faintly as it moved. She drove off toward the woods, hitched Dollie to a tree again. Now for the old folks.

When she reached the cabin, Old Rit and Ben were arguing. Rit said she wasn't going to leave without her feather tick and Ben said she couldn't take it with her. Old Rit appealed to Harriet. "He's got his broadax," she said. "Why can't I take my feather tick? It took me most of my life to get the feathers to make that tick and I'm not going off anywhere without it."

Harriet said, "We'll take it along. But we've got to hurry."

She carried the broadax and the feather tick, loaded them on the wagon and then helped Ben and Old Rit up on the seat. She murmured a prayer under her breath when she untied Dollie. Lord, let this horse hold out or we'll never make it.

Then she climbed up on the seat, said, "Giddap," slapped Dollie with the reins and they were off. They traveled all that night. Toward morning, Harriet got off the seat and led Dollie and the wagon off the road. They spent the day in the woods. The old people ate and then went off to sleep. When it got dark they set out again.

Three nights later, just at dusk, Harriet stopped the wagon in front of Thomas Garrett's house in Wilmington. She had got them safely through this far. The rest of the trip would be comparatively easy.

Garrett gave Harriet enough money to take all of them to Canada. From Wilmington on up she followed her usual route, stopping in Philadelphia, and then in New York.

The pattern of her life changed after the rescue of Ben and Old Rit. It was cold in St. Catharines in June, 1857. Old Rit said she did not believe she would ever feel warm again as long as she lived. Ben, too old and tired to use his beloved broadax, said nothing. He hugged the fireside and sighed.

Harriet, listening to them, watching them, doubted that they could survive the winters, and thought with nostalgia of the Tidewater country, and the smell of honeysuckle and the warmth that lay over the land in the month of June, so that the fields, the earth, the woods, yielded and held heat and a thousand fragrances; even after the sun went down, the night air was warm and sweet-smelling.

She wondered what she ought to do. It wouldn't be safe for them to live in the United States. The Fugitive Slave Law was still in force, though there were few people in the North who would willingly betray a fugitive. Yet it was a risky thing to do.

But she had run risks before, plenty of them. One way or another, she had been running risks all her life. They ought to be fairly safe in New York state. Frederick Douglass lived in Rochester, Jarm Loguen lived in Syracuse; both men were friends of hers. But her mother and father would find cities like Rochester and Syracuse too big and bewildering, too noisy. She thought of the smaller places, stops on the underground, and remembered Auburn, a small town, with elm trees arching over its streets, and smooth lawn, and houses painted white. It was a friendly place.

In 1857 she bought a small frame house in Auburn from William H. Seward, who was at the time the United States Senator from New York. The house was at the end of South Street, beyond

178

the tollgate, on land that belonged to Senator Seward. She had very little money to make a down payment, so there was a rather large mortgage.

That fall she was back in Dorchester County, Maryland, again. In October, William Still recorded the arrival of sixty fugitives from the area in and around Cambridge. All of them had followed the Underground Railroad route under Harriet's direction though she did not go with them all the way to Philadelphia.

But she spent the winter of 1857–58 in St. Catharines, working in the woods, cooking, cleaning, doing whatever jobs she could get.

During those winter months she was troubled by a recurrent, disturbing dream which had no meaning. Night after night she dreamed that she was "in a wilderness sort of place, all full of rocks and bushes." Very slowly, the head of a snake appeared on the rocks, and as she looked, terrified, the head changed, and turned into the head of an old man with a long white beard and glittering eyes. He kept looking, "wishful like, just as if he was going to speak to me." Slowly two other heads appeared beside his. These were smaller heads, and the faces were younger. Suddenly a crowd of men came swarming over the rocks and struck down the heads of the two young men and then the head of the old man. All the time he kept looking at her as though he wanted to say something to her and couldn't.

One day, in April, she went deep into the woods to gather firewood. When she finished, she sat down on a rock to rest. She looked up and saw a man approaching her. In the distance he looked like an old man, his shoulders stooped, but he walked with the swift space-covering gait of a young man.

When she saw his face, she drew in her breath. It was the face of the old man in her dreams, the same white beard, the glittering gray-blue eyes. Then Jarm Loguen came up to them. He told Harriet that the man looking at her with such interest was John Brown, and that he had come a long distance just to meet her and talk with her.

She listened to Brown in silence. He wanted her to tell him the route she had followed on the way North from Maryland, to reveal the hiding places she had used in the swamps, the forests, all the secrets she had learned in the last eight years, in those trips back and forth through the Tidewater country.

He said that he needed this information because he was going to free the slaves, on a large scale. He planned to establish himself in a stronghold in the mountains of Virginia. Once having done that, the slaves would rise up and flock to him. He would arm them with pikes and guns so that they could fight for their freedom. He wanted her to join him in this project so that she could lead the slaves to Canada. He also wanted her to help him here in Canada in raising recruits for the small army of men that he would need for this enterprise.

As he talked she thought of Nat Turner. And she was repelled by the thought of the bloodshed that must inevitably take place, remembering Nat and the bloody swath he had left behind him that night in Virginia, all those years ago, when he too had decided the time had come to free the slaves. This old man, like Nat, worshiped a God of wrath, of vengeance. The God she worshiped was a God of infinite mercy, of gentleness.

Yet his sincerity made a deep impression on her. He was so in earnest. He shared her hatred of slavery, shared her belief that freeedom was a right all men should enjoy, and yet— She hesitated.

Finally she said she would help him. Later on, she suggested a possible date for the beginning of this action—the Fourth of July.

While in St. Catharines, John Brown wrote a letter to his son, John Brown, Jr., reporting on the success of his Canadian trip: "April 8, 1858. . . . I am succeeding to all appearance, beyond my expectation. Harriet Tubman hooked on his [her] whole team at once. He [she] is the most of man, naturally, that I ever met with. There is the most abundant material, and of the right quality, in this quarter, beyond all doubt. . . ."

But Harriet, waiting in St. Catharines, waiting for further word from John Brown, heard nothing.

In March, 1857, Buchanan was inaugurated President of the United States. A few days later, Chief Justice Roger B. Taney delivered the Supreme Court decision in the Dred Scott case. The Court said that: Scott was not a person or a citizen but a piece of slave property that must be returned to slavery; the Missouri Compromise was unconstitutional and therefore slavery could not be forbidden in the Territories.

In Springfield, Illinois, Abraham Lincoln said: "We think the decision is erroneous. We know the Court that made it has often overruled its own decisions, and we shall do what we can to have it overrule this."

On November 13, 1858, The National Anti-Slavery Standard, *published in New York, made the following comment on a convention of slaveholders held in Cambridge, Maryland:*

"The operation of the Underground Railroad on the Maryland border, within the last few years has been so extensive that in some neighborhoods the whole slave population have made their escape, and the Convention is a result of the general panic on the part of the owners of this specie of property . . ."

Though the Standard *carefully avoided all mention of Harriet Tubman's name, it was a recognized fact in Abolitionist circles that she was responsible for the panic. Under her guidance, over three hundred slaves had reached the North and freedom. By 1860 the rewards offered for her capture totaled sixty thousand dollars.*

20. The Lecture Platform

HARRIET SPENT most of the winter of 1858–1859 in Boston. She was badly in need of funds. There was the mortgage on the house in Auburn, which she never seemed to be able to pay off, no matter how hard she worked, and she wanted to make another trip to Maryland.

By this time she was known by reputation throughout the North. Many people called her "Molly Pitcher" because of the stories they had heard about the daring rescue trips she made into the South. Her friends in New York had urged her to go to Boston—people there were eager to meet her and equally eager to help her.

Early in December 1858 she arrived in Boston, with a little packet of letters of introduction and a small bundle of daguerreotypes—pictures of some of her old friends like Gerrit Smith and Thomas Garrett. That afternoon of her arrival she sat in the front parlor of a boarding house waiting for a man named Franklin B. Sanborn. She had never seen him but he knew some of her friends. One of the letters of introduction she had brought from New York was addressed to him.

She felt a little strange in Boston. She never thought of her own safety. It was just that this city was unlike New York or Philadelphia or Syracuse or any other city she had known. The streets were very narrow and as crooked as a hickory stick. Most of them were cobbled. From what little she had seen of this famous old city, it looked like a place where it would be easy to get lost.

She folded her hands in her lap and her lips curved into a smile. Why would she get lost here? She had traveled thousands of miles and never lost her sense of direction. Suddenly she frowned. How would she recognize Mr. Sanborn? Suppose some slave catcher came instead. Boston was said to be overrun with them.

Then there was a tap on the door of the parlor. She said, "Come in," and stood up, holding herself very straight. The tall man who entered, smiled, said, "Mrs. Tubman?" and when she nodded, said, "I'm Franklin Sanborn."

She did not answer him. Instead she opened the little package of pictures that she had placed on a table near her chair and handed one of them to him. Because it had occurred to her that if he recognized the picture, then surely he was who he said he was—Franklin B. Sanborn. In the back of her mind an old memory flared: the Sims boy, Anthony Burns, Shadrach, all of them arrested here in Boston, charged with being fugitives. And she was a fugitive, too. For all she knew, this big young man smiling at her with such cordiality might be a sheriff—or—

"Do you know who that is?" she asked.

He raised his eyebrows. "It's Gerrit Smith," he said. "Why do you ask?"

When she explained, he nodded, his eyes amused. "You're quite right to be cautious." As she continued to stand, he said, "Let's sit down and talk."

He sat down beside her, asked her a few questions, listened intently as she answered, kept her talking—for more than an hour. As he was leaving he asked her if she would make a speech at an anti-slavery meeting in about two weeks. At first she refused. But he overrode her objections, saying, "You have no idea how important it is that you should tell some of these stories to the people here in Boston."

Two weeks later there she was on the platform at Faneuil Hall. She was wearing a dark gray long-skirted cotton dress. The only adornment was a bit of lace at the neck and jet buttons down the front. She held an old black reticule on her lap. The other speakers were distinguished-looking men: Wendell Phillips, Franklin Sanborn, Thomas Wentworth Higginson.

When Sanborn introduced her, she stood looking shyly at this audience of well-dressed people, not knowing what to say. And someone on the platform asked her a question, and then another. Then she started talking, telling about the trips she had made back into the slave country, how she carefully selected the slaves that would go North with her, how they traveled mostly on foot, wading through rivers, hiding in haystacks, in barns. Sometimes there were babies in the party, and once when there were twin infants, tiny babies that she had drugged with opium so that they would sleep, she found that one of the stopping places on the route had a new and hostile owner. She had expected to find food and shelter for her passengers and instead had to hurry them along, hungry, cold, fearful, and she herself fearful, too.

She had led them to the edge of a swamp, and she remembered there was an island in the swamp, so she took them there, leading them through the tall rank swamp grass, urging them on, because the people at the farm where she had stopped might well spread the word that a group of runaways was in the neighborhood. She had them lie down in the swampy grass, so tall it concealed them completely. It was cold there on that sedgy little island, and they shivered, their clothes sodden with mud; only the babies, the little twins, were dry and warm in their basket. She said she looked at them, looked at their small brown fists, and thought of them as treasures, tiny treasures who would be free with the help of the Lord.

They stayed there all day. All day she prayed, "Lord, I'm going to hold steady on to You—" There was always danger on the road, always the unexpected, but the Lord had never failed her.

The sun began to go down, and the tall grass looked golden. Then the light began to fade and water birds murmured their good night songs. It was dusk, and the little island was all shadow, when she saw a man. He was walking up and down along the edge of the swamp. She frowned, watching him, wondering what he was doing there. He could not possibly see them. He wore the wide-brimmed hat of a Quaker, and she thought perhaps he is really a friend, and yet one could never be sure. Anyone could put on the clothes of a Quaker, a Quaker's clothing did not turn a man into a friend.

His lips kept moving. She thought he must be talking to himself. She listened, and she heard what he said:

"My wagon stands in the barnyard of the next farm, right across the way. The horse is in the stable. The harness hangs on a nail."

He repeated these words. Then he was gone as suddenly as he had come.

When it was completely dark, Harriet left the little island, moving slowly, quietly. She looked back. The tall grass concealed where her passengers lay. No one passing by would know that they were there. They did not move, did not talk.

She approached the farm as cautiously and as quietly as she had left the island, a prayer on her lips. Sure enough there was a wagon, a big farm wagon in the barnyard. She reached inside it, felt along it, to make certain that no one lay concealed in it. One never knew when one might be walking straight into a trap of some kind. Her hands touched something bulky and she gave an exclamation of surprise. There was a package on the floor of the wagon, bulky. She pulled it toward her, and almost cried from thankfulness, for she could smell food.

187

After that she moved quickly into the barn. A big white horse turned his head toward her, and she patted him, then put on the harness. A few minutes later she had hitched him to the wagon and was driving toward the little island. Thus she and her passengers rode to the next stop on the road (the Underground Railroad), a farm belonging to another Quaker, where they left the horse and wagon to be picked up by its owner.

She described the rest of the journey, the stop at Thomas Garrett's in Wilmington, and the slow journey North to Philadelphia, where William Still recorded their names and the names of their owners in his thick notebook.

This firsthand information about the Underground Railroad, by a woman who had served as one of its conductors, thrilled that first audience before whom she spoke. They stood on their feet and cheered and clapped when she finished.

After that first speech she was a much sought-after speaker in Boston and its environs. Her appearance had undergone subtle changes during the course of the years. There was something brooding and tender in her face, a gentleness in her eyes. The lips were slightly compressed, the only indication of a never quite fulfilled hunger for affection. Her speaking voice, deep in pitch, slightly husky, was more beautiful than ever. Yet sometimes she sat on a platform in plain sight of an audience and went sound asleep just as she had often done on the long road to the North. In spite of this strange handicap, she was a tremendously successful public speaker.

During that winter in Boston, she saw John Brown several times. He called himself Captain Smith because he did not want his enemies to know his whereabouts. Harriet told him all she knew of the routes to the North, the hiding places on the way out of Maryland, drawing crude maps for him. During the spring and early summer she waited for further word from him, and heard nothing more.

She was much in demand as a speaker. She visited Concord, Framingham, Worcester, speaking at antislavery meetings.

Early in June, Thomas Wentworth Higginson told her that he had had a letter from Franklin Sanborn. And that Sanborn had said John Brown "is desirous of getting someone to go to Canada and collect recruits for him among the fugitives . . . with H. [Harriet] Tubman, or alone. . . ."

Higginson told her that he had lost confidence in the plan. He said that it had "grown rather vague and dubious" in his mind because of the repeated postponements.

Harriet did not know what to think. The Fourth of July had come and gone. On that day she made a speech at a meeting of the Massachusetts Anti-Slavery Society at Framingham. Someone said that Brown was in Maryland, and someone else said, no, he was in New York.

On the 1st of August she was back in Boston to make another speech. She liked Boston. Whenever she had a moment's leisure she went to Boston

Common. Sanborn had told her something of its history, said that years ago a Quaker, a woman, had been hanged there and that a mob once tried to hang William Lloyd Garrison there. Sanborn said that these days all manner of people aired their grievances on Boston Common. He spoke of Amelia Bloomer, and laughed, describing the costume she had worn when she made a speech there one afternoon. She had on full, stiff trousers that reached all the way to her ankles and were tied there. He said it was one of the funniest sights he'd ever seen.

Harriet thought that over, and though she did not say so, decided that she could have used just such a costume many times. Long, full skirts would hamper any woman who had walked and ridden along a road that almost ran under the ground.

Harriet never heard from John Brown again, never saw him again. She was unaware of the fact that Brown and his assistants kept referring to her in the letters that they sent to the Boston Abolitionists who were helping to finance his project. "Harriet Tubman is probably in New Bedford, sick. She has staid in N.E. [New England] a long time. And been a kind of missionary." "I have sent a note to Harriet requesting her to come to Boston." "When Harriet comes. . . ."

But Harriet never came. Perhaps she was ill, perhaps Higginson had told her that he had lost confidence in the plan, perhaps word of Frederick Douglass's absolute refusal to enter what he believed to be a steel trap had influenced her—in any event, she was not at Harper's Ferry, nor did she send any recruits from Canada.

On October 17, 1859, she was in New York, visiting friends. It had been years since she had experienced that curious fluttering sensation of her heart, a wild beating inside her chest, that she interpreted as a warning of danger. But that morning, at the breakfast table, she held her hands against her chest. She said, "Something's wrong. Something dreadful has happened, or is about to happen."

Her hostess looked about the dining room, white tablecloth on the table, pretty china sprinkled with rosebuds, the good smell of bacon in the room, and the fragrance of coffee, and shook her head. "But Harriet," she protested, "there's always something wrong somewhere."

Harriet frowned and closed her eyes, thinking, wondering. Then she shivered, feeling suddenly cold. "It's Captain Brown," she said. "Something is happening to him. Something dreadful has happened to him."

No argument could shake off her feeling of disaster. Later in the day they heard that the United States Government Arsenal at Harper's Ferry had been seized. The next day's papers carried the news: eighteen men in the fire-engine house with Brown, ten of them were killed, including two of Brown's sons. John Brown had been taken prisoner.

A week later, Old John Brown was put on trial. He was found guilty and sentenced to death.

Harriet was deeply affected by Brown's death.

She worshiped his memory. It seemed to her amazing that a white man, free, independent, should have held such strong convictions on the subject of slavery that he was willing to risk his life in order that slaves should be free.

Someone read her the final statement that he made. She had it read to her over and over again, until she knew parts of it by heart: ". . . I say I am yet too young to understand that God is any respecter of persons. . . . I believe that to have interfered as I have done, as I have always freely admitted I have done, in behalf of His despised poor, I did no wrong but right. . . ."

Harriet always regretted that he had not made his plans more carefully. The slaves in the area had no knowledge of his intention, had been given not so much as a hint that such a plan existed, or that it in any way involved them, and they were as disturbed and frightened by the action at Harper's Ferry as the rest of the country.

She resolved to do something in memory of Captain John Brown, something, she did not know what, "in behalf of God's despised poor."

John Brown was hanged at Charlestown, Virginia, on the 2nd of December, 1859. A rope made of South Carolina long staple cotton was displayed outside the jail. The placard above it read: "No Northern hemp shall help to punish our felony."

He became a ghost and a legend that haunted both North and South.

In 1859 The Richmond Whig *said: "The miser-*

able old traitor and murderer belongs to the gallows and the gallows will have its own."

In Boston, Wendell Phillips, Abolitionist and reformer, commended those who looked "upon that gibbet of John Brown, not as the scaffold of a felon, but as the cross of a martyr."

21. With the Union Army

AFTER THE DEATH of John Brown, Harriet began to feel dissatisfied with the life she was leading. It seemed to her that she was doing absolutely nothing for the cause of freedom. Certainly the audiences before whom she spoke offered no challenge to her ingenuity or her imagination. She traveled on trains unhampered, unhindered, stayed in boarding houses or visited the homes of her friends, openly, freely. When she thought of the restrictions imposed on the slave population, she longed to return to Maryland to bring out more slaves.

She was still surprised by the enthusiastic reception she was accorded. When she finished talking, people began to clap, and then they stood and cheered, and came up to the platform to shake hands with her, to give her money. Many of them told her not to make any more trips into the South for fear she would be caught.

This was a thought that she impatiently rejected as of no consequence. She was more interested in how the whole question of slavery would be settled. She was certain that it would be settled soon—one way or another. Southerners believed that the entire North had supported John Brown and in 1860 they lived in dread because they thought that a tremendous uprising of the slaves might still occur. Northerners, as far as she could tell from what she saw and heard in her travels, had turned the Fugitive Slave Law into a joke. People said that in northern Ohio, where Levi Coffin operated the busiest branch of the Underground Railroad, it was impossible to put an Abolitionist in jail and keep him there, no matter how guilty he might be of harboring runaways.

It was almost impossible to try a runaway slave. She found that out herself, because she became involved in the case of a runaway slave who had been arrested and was to be tried.

On April 27, 1860, she was in Troy, New York. She had spent the night there and was going on to Boston to attend an antislavery meeting. That morning she was on her way to the railroad station. She walked along the street slowly. She never bothered to find out when a train was due, she simply sat in the station and waited until a train came which was going in the direction she desired.

It was cold in Troy even though it was the spring of the year. A northeast wind kept blowing the ruffle on her bonnet away from her face. She thought of Maryland and how green the trees would be. Here they were only lightly touched with green, not yet in full leaf. Suddenly she longed for a sight of the Eastern Shore with its coves and creeks, thought of the years that had elapsed since she first ran away from there.

She stopped walking to watch a crowd of people in front of the courthouse, a pushing, shoving, shouting crowd. She wondered what had happened. A fight? An accident? She went nearer, listened to the loud excited voices. "He got away." "He didn't." "They've got him handcuffed." Then there was an eruptive movement, people pushing forward, other people pushing back.

Harriet started working her way through the crowd, elbowing a man, nudging a woman. Now and then she asked a question. She learned that a runaway slave named Charles Nalle had been arrested and was being taken inside the courthouse to be tried.

When she finally got close enough to see the runaway's face, a handsome frightened face, his guards had forced him up the courthouse steps. They were trying to get through the door but people blocked the way.

She knew a kind of fury against the system, against the men who would force this man back into slavery when they themselves were free. The Lord did not intend that people should be slaves, she thought. Then without even thinking, she went up the steps, forced her way through the crowd, until she stood next to Nalle.

There was a small boy standing near her, mouth open, eyes wide with curiosity. She grabbed him by the collar and whispered to him fiercely, "You go out in the street and holler 'Fire, fire' as loud as you can."

The crowd kept increasing and she gave a nod of satisfaction. That little boy must have got out there in the street and must still be hollering that there's a fire. She bent over, making her shoulders droop, bending her back in the posture of an old woman. She pulled her sunbonnet way down, so that it shadowed her face. Just in time, too. One of the policemen said, "Old woman, you'll have to get out of here. You're liable to get knocked down when we take him through the door."

Harriet moved away from Nalle, mumbling to herself. She heard church bells ringing somewhere in the distance, and more and more people came running. The entire street was blocked. She edged back toward Nalle. Suddenly she shouted, "Don't let them take him! Don't let them take him!"

She attacked the nearest policeman so suddenly that she knocked him down. She wanted to laugh at the look of surprise on his face when he realized that the mumbling old woman who had stood so close to him had suddenly turned into a creature of vigor and violence. Grabbing Nalle by the arm, she pulled him along with her, forcing her way down the steps, ignoring the blows she received, not really feeling them, taking pleasure in the fact that in all these months of inactivity she had lost none of her strength.

When they reached the street they were both knocked down. Harriet snatched off her bonnet and tied it on Nalle's head. When they stood up it was impossible to pick him out of the crowd. People in the street cleared a path for them, helped hold back the police. As they turned off the main street, they met a man driving a horse and wagon. He reined in the horse. "What goes on here?" he asked.

Harriet, out of breath, hastily explained the situation. The man got out of the wagon. "Here," he said, "use my horse and wagon. I don't care if I ever get it back just so that man gets to safety."

Nalle was rapidly driven to Schenectady and from there he went on to the West—and safety.

Harriet's friends knew that she was in danger of arrest for the part she had played in Nalle's rescue. They saw to it that she stayed hidden in a house on the outskirts of Troy for two days.

Shortly afterward she went to Boston where she filled two speaking engagements, one at a meeting of the New England Antislavery Society on May 27th, the other at a women's suffrage meeting on the 1st of June.

After this she returned to Auburn, where she spent the summer. She was restless, impatient. People were talking about Abe Lincoln. He had won the Republican nomination for the presidency in the spring. No one thought he had a chance of winning the election. Even if he did, Harriet doubted that he would do anything about slavery.

In November, 1860, she made another trip to Tidewater Maryland. Perhaps she felt the need for action, perhaps she wanted to return to the fields and the woods and streams of the Eastern Shore, in order to offset the tame-cat life she had been leading on lecture platforms. Possibly the rescue of Charles Nalle had whetted her appetite for adventure. Perhaps the memory of John Brown haunted her, too.

In any event, she brought out a man and his

wife, with three children, one of them six years old, one of them four years old, and a three-months' old baby, and another man. En route to Thomas Garrett's in Wilmington they met a young woman who was also escaping, and she joined the party.

On December 1st, Thomas Garrett wrote one of his characteristic letters to William Still in Philadelphia:

I write to let thee know that Harriet Tubman is again in these parts. She arrived last evening from one of her trips of mercy to God's poor, bringing two men with her as far as New Castle. I agreed to pay a man last evening, to pilot them on their way to Chester county; the wife of one of the men, with two or three children, was left some thirty miles below, and I gave Harriet ten dollars, to hire a man with carriage, to take them to Chester county. She said a man had offered for that sum, to bring them on. I shall be very uneasy about them, till I hear they are safe. There is now much more risk on the road, till they arrive here, than there has been for several months past, as we find that some poor, worthless wretches are constantly on the look out on two roads, that they cannot well avoid more especially with carriage, yet, as it is Harriet who seems to have had

a special angel to guard her on her journey of mercy, I have hope.

Thy Friend,
Thomas Garrett

Despite Garrett's uneasiness, the entire party
arrived safely in Philadelphia. William Still wrote
their names down on loose slips of paper. His big
notebook had been hidden, for "the capture of John
Brown's papers and letters, with names and plans
in full, admonished us that such papers and cor-
respondence as had been preserved concerning the
Underground Rail Road, might perchance be captured by a pro-slavery mob."

Still wrote swiftly and briefly: "Arrival from
Dorchester Co., 1860," and under it, "Harriet Tubman's Last 'Trip' to Maryland." Then he put down
the names of the people who came with her, and
that was all.

When Harriet returned from this trip, her friends
in Auburn hurried her off to Canada, suddenly
afraid for her safety. It was not until she reached
Canada that she learned that Old Abe Lincoln had
won the election in November.

In December, South Carolina seceded from the
Union. As the year turned, the cotton states began
leaving the Union: Mississippi, Florida, Alabama,
Georgia, Louisiana, Texas.

In January, 1861, she was back in Boston. She
was there when John A. Andrew was inaugurated
Governor of Massachusetts. He was a short heavy-

set man who wore spectacles. Men said he was a
Free Soiler and a radical. The day he was inaugurated, he sent out a call for the Massachusetts
Militia, and sent a man to England to see about
guns. He talked about the need for money for overcoats for the militia. That winter on Boston Common, Harriet heard the word "overcoat" become
a joke, a slang word for "warmonger."

In February, the states that had seceded formed
a new union called the Confederate States of
America. Jefferson Davis was elected President of
the Confederacy. On April 14th, the Confederacy
took over Fort Sumter. Lincoln sent out a call for
militia.

Governor John A. Andrew of Massachusetts
telegraphed the President, "The quota of troops
required of Massachusetts is ready. How will you
have them proceed?" The answer was, "Send them
by rail."

No other state in the Union was prepared to act
so quickly. In a week's time, Massachusetts was
able to send out infantry, riflemen and artillery,
properly equipped and thoroughly drilled.

It was John Andrew, the dimpled, curly-headed
Governor of Massachusetts, who was responsible
for Harriet Tubman's final major role. During the
Civil War she became a scout, a spy, a nurse for
the Union forces. In May, 1862, she boarded the
Atlantic, a Government transport, headed for Beaufort, which is located on Port Royal, one of the Sea
Islands, off the coast of South Carolina. She was

sent there at the recommendation of Governor Andrew.

The Confederate forts had been taken on November 7, 1861, and Port Royal and St. Helena were being used by the Union Army as supply stations. Slaves had been flocking to these islands ever since the Union forces had set up headquarters there. These slaves were referred to as "contrabands." The term originated from an army report of May 24, 1861. Three fugitives were brought into Fortress Monroe by the Union picket guard. The Confederates asked for their rendition under the terms of the Fugitive Slave Law, but they were informed by General Butler that "under the peculiar circumstances, he considered the fugitives 'contraband' of war."

Port Royal was filled with contrabands, poverty-stricken, sick, homeless, starving. Many of them had traveled miles from the interior of South Carolina in order to reach the Union headquarters on the island. Some of them had been wounded by plantation owners who had attempted to halt their flight. A hospital had been set up for them on Port Royal.

It was in this contraband hospital that Harriet Tubman began to play her new role of nurse. She said, "I'd go to the hospital, I would, early every morning. I'd get a big chunk of ice, I would, and put it in a basin, and fill it with water; then I'd take a sponge and begin. First man I'd come to, I'd thrash away the flies, and they'd rise, they would, like bees around a hive. Then I'd begin to bathe the wounds, and by the time I bathed off three or four, the fire and heat would have melted the ice and made the water warm, and it would be as red as clear blood. Then I'd go and get more ice, I would, and by the time I got to the next ones, the flies would be around the first ones black and thick as ever."

More deadly than the wounds was the dysentery. Each morning when she went back to the hospital, she found more and more people had died from it. She was certain she could check it if she could find the same roots and herbs here on the island that had grown in Maryland. But this was a strange new country to her; even the plant life was different.

One night she went into a wooded area, near the water, and searched until she found the great white flowers of the water lily floating on the surface, reached down and pulled up the roots, hunted until she found crane's bill. Then she went back to the small house where she lived and boiled the roots and herbs, making a strange dark-looking concoction. It was a bitter-tasting brew. But it worked. The next morning she gave it to a man who was obviously dying, and slowly he got better.

Once again men called her Moses, saying that no one could die if Moses was at the bedside.

She soon learned, however, that the contrabands resented her being able to draw rations, as though she were an officer or a soldier. They saw no reason why she should be so especially privileged. So she stopped drawing rations. In order to earn money to buy food with, she made pies at night, and a home-brewed root-beer, which she got one of the contrabands to peddle in the nearby army camps during the day.

In January, 1863, shortly after Lincoln had proclaimed the slaves free, she saw a regiment of Negro soldiers for the first time. Thomas Wentworth Higginson, their commanding officer, was an old friend of Harriet's. As Harriet watched these men parade through the sandy streets, shaded by the tremendous live oaks, one thousand ex-slaves marching in unison, she was overcome by emotion. The band of the Eighth Maine met the regiment at the entrance to Beaufort and escorted them all the way.

She thought this the most moving sight she had ever beheld: a regiment of black, newly freed South Carolinians wearing the uniform of the Union forces, escorted by the band of a white regiment. She knew how Sergeant Prince Rivers, the six-foot color sergeant of the First Carolina Volunteers, felt when he said, "And when that band wheel in before us, and march on—my God! I quit this world altogether."

That night, long after she'd gone to bed, she could hear a kind of rhythmic hum from the direction of the camp—sound of singing, the clapping of hands, the throbbing of drums, a kind of carry-over of the day's excitement.

About a month later, she started serving as a scout for Colonel James Montgomery, who had encamped at Port Royal with the first detachment of the Second South Carolina Volunteers, also composed of ex-slaves. On the night of June 2, 1863, Harriet accompanied Montgomery and his men in a raid up the Combahee River. They had two objectives: to destroy or take up the torpedoes that the enemy had placed in the Combahee and to bring back to Port Royal as many contrabands as they could entice away from the river area.

They soon found out that they would not have to entice the inhabitants away. As the gunboats went farther and farther up the Combahee, they began to see slaves working in the rice fields. At first the slaves ran away, toward the woods. Then the word was passed around, "Lincoln's gunboats done come to set us free."

People started coming toward the boats, coming down the paths, through the meadows, for on each side of the river there were rice fields and slaves working in them. They kept coming, with bundles on their heads, children riding on their mothers' shoulders, all of them ragged, dirty, the children naked.

Harriet said that she had never seen anything like it before. "Here you'd see a woman with a pail on her head, rice a-smoking in it just as she'd taken it from the fire, young one hanging on behind, one hand round her forehead to hold on, other hand digging into the ricepot, eating with all its might, hold of her dress two or three more; down her back a bag with a pig in it.

"One woman brought two pigs, a white one and a black one; we took them all on board; named the white pig Beauregard, and the black pig Jeff Davis. Sometimes the women would come with twins hanging round their necks; appears like I never see so many twins in my life; bags on their shoulders, baskets on their heads, and young ones tagging behind, all loaded; pigs squealing, chickens screaming, young ones squalling."

They were taken off the shore in rowboats. All the contrabands tried to get in the small boats at once. Even after the boats were crowded, they clung to the sides of them, holding them fast to the shore. The men rowing the boats struck at their hands with the oars, but they would not let go. They were afraid they would be left behind.

Finally Montgomery shouted from the deck of one of the gunboats, "Moses, you'll have to give 'em a song."

Harriet sang:

Of all the whole creation in the East or in the West,
The glorious Yankee nation is the greatest and the best.
Come along! Come along! don't be alarmed,
Uncle Sam is rich enough to give you all a farm.

As each verse ended, the contrabands threw up their hands and shouted, "Glory! Glory! Glory!" Immediately the small boats pulled off. Hurriedly unloading their passengers on the decks of the gunboats, they came back and got more. After the small boats were filled, Harriet had to sing again and again until they got all 750 contrabands on board.

Shortly afterward, Harriet had someone write a letter to Franklin B. Sanborn in Boston, asking for a bloomer dress because long skirts were a handicap on an expedition.

Sanborn was at that time editor of *The Boston Commonwealth*. He made a front-page story of the Combahee raid, and Harriet's part in it. It appeared Friday, July 10, 1863: "Col. Montgomery and his gallant band of 300 black soldiers, under the guidance of a black woman, dashed into the enemy's country, struck a bold and effective blow . . . and brought off near 800 slaves. . . ."

"Since the rebellion she [Harriet] has devoted herself to her great work of delivering the bondman, with an energy and sagacity that cannot be exceeded. Many and many times she has penetrated the enemy's lines and discovered their situation and condition, and escaped without injury, but not without extreme hazard. . . ."

During the winter of 1859–60 when Abraham Lincoln was campaigning for the Republicans in the New England states, he spoke of the reason for the difference in the point of view of the South and the North. In Hartford, Connecticut, he said: "One-sixth of the population of the United States are slaves, looked upon as property, as nothing but property. The cash value of these slaves, at a moderate estimate, is two billion dollars. This amount of property value has a vast influence on the minds of its owners, very naturally. The same amount of property would have an equal influence upon us if owned in the North. Human nature is the same— people at the South are the same as those at the North, barring the difference in circumstances. . . ."

22. *The Last Years*

IN THE SPRING of 1864, Harriet went back to Auburn to rest, to visit with Old Rit and Ben. She had been with the Military Department of the South for two years. She brought home a bundle of letters and passes with her. There was one dated July 6, 1863, from Colonel Montgomery to General Gilmore, who was in command of the Department of the South. Montgomery had referred to her as "a most remarkable woman, and invaluable as a scout."

Another document, written by General David Hunter, February 19, 1863, said: "Pass the bearer, Harriet Tubman, to Beaufort and back to this place, and wherever she wishes to go; and give her free passage at all times, on all Government transports. Harriet was sent to me from Boston by Governor Andrew, of Massachusetts, and is a valuable woman. She has permission, as a servant of the Government, to purchase such provisions from the Commissary as she may need." This was countersigned by General Gilmore, who took Hunter's place as commander of the Department of the South.

Before she left Port Royal, Henry K. Durrant, the surgeon in charge of the Contraband Hospital, presented her with a certificate dated at Beaufort, South Carolina, May 3, 1864: "I certify that I have been acquainted with Harriet Tubman for nearly two years; and my position as Medical Officer in charge of 'contrabands' in this town and in hospital, has given me frequent and ample opportunities to observe her general deportment; particularly her kindness and attention to the sick and suffering of her own race. I take much pleasure in testifying to the esteem in which she is generally held." General Saxton added a note: "I concur fully in the above."

Harriet stayed in Auburn for a year. During the summer she paid a visit to Boston. The following spring she was in Washington, for she intended to return to Port Royal. She even received a War Department order providing for transportation there, dated at Washington, March 20, 1865: "Pass Mrs. Harriet Tubman (colored) to Hilton Head and Charleston, S.C., with free transportation on a Gov't transport. By order of Sec. of War." This was signed by Louis H. Pelonge, "Asst. Agt. Gener'l." But instead of returning to the Department of the South, she worked in the Contraband Hospital at Fortress Monroe. She was there when the war ended on April 9, 1865.

On April 2nd, Grant took Petersburg. A week later, April 9th, Lee surrendered to him at Appomattox Courthouse. Grant said afterward, in his *Personal Memoirs,* "I felt like anything rather than rejoicing at the downfall of a foe who had fought so long, and valiantly, and had suffered so much for a cause, though that cause was, I believe, one of the worst for which a people ever fought and one for which there was the least excuse. . . ."

Six nights after Lee's surrender, Lincoln was shot by John Wilkes Booth. He died the next morning, April 15, 1865.

Harriet stayed at Fortress Monroe until July of 1865. Then she went back to Auburn, New York. The war had been over nearly four months. She was tired. Old Rit and Ben needed her.

With the ratification of the Thirteenth Amendment to the Constitution in December, the long period of agitation for the abolition of slavery came to an end. Like many others who in one way or another had worked toward that goal, Harriet was at a loss as to what to do next. She sought for a new cause, and never really found one. Like many other former Abolitionists, she became interested in the movement for women's suffrage. She helped raise money for schools for the newly freed slaves. She farmed a little, raising fruit and vegetables, looked after Old Rit and Ben, and offered food and shelter to any homeless wanderer who needed a place to stay. She made repeated efforts to obtain some kind of remuneration for her service with the Union forces. Her friends wrote letters for her, presented petitions to Congressional committees— and nothing came of it.

It must have seemed a terribly tame existence to a woman who so recently had carried a musket and a canteen and a haversack on scouting expeditions through the marshes and along the river banks of the South Carolina Low Country; and who, in the years when she was a conductor on the Underground Railroad, had waded through rivers, and been jounced around in the bottom of farm wagons, had hidden in haystacks, and listened, holding her breath, to the hoofbeats of the patrollers, in the Tidewater country in Maryland.

Sometimes she experienced moments of regret for the one thing she had never had: the home complete with a husband and children. One day in October, 1867, she was assailed by the memory of herself as a young girl—a field hand, slowly piecing together a patchwork quilt, her fingers clumsy at first, unaccustomed to holding a needle—because she learned of the death of John Tubman to whom she had been married. He was murdered in Talbot County, Maryland, on the road to Airey. There was a brief news item about it in the *Baltimore American*. She could not help thinking how different her life would have been if she and John had lived together, somewhere in the North, and had had children.

When she heard of John's death, she felt old and lonely. True, the people in Auburn liked her, admired her. They knew she had little or no money, had to support her old parents as best she could, knew that she could never turn away from her door anyone who said that he had no home, needed food, needed help, and so always had a larger household than one woman could hope to feed and clothe. The neighbors brought food to the little house on South Street—a bag of flour, a sack of potatoes, or a basket of apples. Friendly people.

In May of 1868, one of Harriet's friends and admirers, Mrs. Sarah Hopkins Bradford, a school-teacher who lived in Auburn, decided to do something to raise some money for her. She began to write the story of Harriet's life. Most of the direct quotations used by biographers of Harriet Tubman are possible only because of Mrs. Bradford, who first recorded them.

Mrs. Bradford's book, *Scenes in the Life of Harriet Tubman,* appeared early in 1869. On January 9th *The Boston Commonwealth,* in announcing its publication, said that the proceeds from the sale of the biography were to go to Harriet, "she now being very old and infirm." Harriet was, however, neither old nor infirm. She was not more than forty-nine. She was simply a reformer without a cause, and therefore lost, and lonely, and exhausted.

She received twelve hundred dollars from the sale of the book. She paid off the mortgage on her house, for she was still in debt to Senator Seward for it. She even had money left over afterward. But she regretted that it came too late for Ben and Old Rit, her mother and father, to benefit by it. They were both dead by then.

In March of that year, she married again. Her husband, Nelson Davis, was more than twenty years younger than she. The folk in Auburn said Harriet had married him in order to take care of him, that even though he was a big, handsome, young man, he had tuberculosis. He had contracted it during the war. He was a veteran who had fought at Olustee, Boykin's Mill, Honey Hill, with the Eighth United States Colored Infantry Volunteers.

True or not, he was obviously unable to contribute to the support of the household on South Street where he lived with Harriet. The supply of money there never wholly met the need for it. And so, in 1886, Mrs. Bradford came to Harriet's rescue for the second time. She wrote another small volume about Harriet, entitled *Harriet, the Moses of Her People*. Again any money from the book was to go to Harriet, who now wanted to found a home for the aged and infirm.

In the preface, Professor Samuel Miles Hopkins (Mrs. Bradford's brother) of Auburn Theological Seminary, said: "Her [Harriet's] household is very likely to consist of several old black people, 'bad with the rheumatiz,' some forlorn wandering woman, and a couple of small images of God cut in ebony. How she manages to feed and clothe herself and them, the Lord best knows. She has too much pride and too much faith to beg. . . ." This certainly suggests that Nelson Davis, Harriet's husband, was unable to make much of a financial contribution to the little house on South Street.

Nelson Davis died on October 14, 1888. He was forty-four years old. Though Harriet had repeatedly applied for a pension for herself or back pay to reimburse her for those years she had served with the Union forces, her claim was never allowed. But in 1899 she was awarded a pension of twenty dollars a month, not for her own services, but as "the

widow of Nelson Davis, who served in Company
G, Eighth United States Infantry, from September
1863, to November 1865, and was honorably dis-
charged."

As she grew older, the pattern of her life changed
again. Finally, she became a tiny little old woman,
peddling vegetables from door to door in Auburn.
She didn't make many stops in the course of a day.
There wasn't time. At each house, she was invited
inside, told to sit down, and urged to tell a story
about some phase of her life. Sometimes she spent
the whole morning in one house. The housewife
who sat across the kitchen table from Harriet,
listening, felt as though she were traveling, too, and
so was reluctant to let her go on to her next stop.

It was as the storyteller, the bard, that Harriet's
active years came to a close. She had never learned
to read and write. She compensated for this handicap by developing a memory on which was indeli-
bly stamped everything she had ever heard or seen or
experienced. She had a highly developed sense of
the dramatic, a sense of the comic, and because in
her early years she had memorized verses from the
Bible, word for word, the surge and sway of the
majestic rhythm of the King James version of the
Bible was an integral part of her speech. It was
these qualities that made her a superb storyteller.

In each house where she stopped, she was given
a cup of hot tea with butter in it, which was the
way she liked it. As she sipped the buttered tea,
she would sometimes tell about the Underground
Railroad, and that first trip she made to Canada,

and how all of them were ragged, hungry, dirty, cold and afraid. Hunger worse than cold, the pinching of the stomach, pain in the stomach, from hunger. And fear worse than hunger, fear like a paralysis, inhibiting movement, fear so strong it was something they could feel and taste. She, threatening, cajoling, admonishing them: "Go free or die."

She made her listener see the snow in Canada, the trees hung with icicles, see Niagara Falls like frozen music in the winter. And she invariably ended the recital with a note of pride in her voice, as she said: "And I never run my train off the track, and I never lost a single passenger."

Sometimes she told about Colonel Robert Gould Shaw, the slender fair-haired boy (he was twenty-six), descendant of one of Boston's oldest and most aristocratic families, who had commanded a regiment of black men, the Fifty-Fourth Massachusetts. She told about how he led the attack on Wagner, how he stood on the parapet waving that sword which had been made in England, a field-officer's sword, with his initials worked in the handle, shouting, "Forward, Fifty-Fourth!" determined to prove the bravery of his regiment, to prove that black men would fight no matter what the odds, and then pitched forward, dead, his sergeant beside him.

Harriet's low-pitched husky voice made Shaw live again. The housewife, bending toward her, lips parted, listening, could see young Shaw, could see the silver eagles on his shoulders, the silk sash around his waist, the light blue of his trousers, the high felt army hat on his head.

Her voice was the voice of an old lady, but it was still beautiful, still thrilling as she summarized the attack on Wagner, summarized all battles by saying, "And then we saw the lightning, and that was the guns; and then we heard the rain falling, and that was the drops of blood falling; and when we came to get in the crops, it was dead men that we reaped."

She could speak of the death of Lincoln, and epitomize all the sorrow in the world by telling about an old man, at the Contraband Hospital at Fortress Monroe, who, hearing that Lincoln was dead, lifted his tremulous old voice in prayer: "We kneel upon the ground, with our faces in our hands, and our hands in the dust, and cry to Thee for mercy, O Lord, this evening."

Sometimes she talked about Old John Brown, the man with the hawk's face and the white beard, and the fanatic's eyes, cold and hard as granite. She told about the time Old Brown took her to see Wendell Phillips and when he introduced her, he said, "Mr. Phillips, I bring you one of the bravest people on this continent—*General* Tubman, as we call her."

Then again she spoke of Port Royal and the contrabands, and the strange speech of the Gullahs of South Carolina, and told about how they had said their masters had told them the Yankees had hoofs, horns and tails, and would sell them to Cuba, how they called the Confederates *secesh*

217

buckra (white men who were secessionists). She showed her passes, those precious pieces of paper that she could not read though she knew by heart what each one of them said, a little bundle of much-fingered, well-worn paper, many of the documents barely decipherable they had been handled so much.

When she spoke of Port Royal, on a cold winter's morning, sitting in the kitchen of a frame house in Auburn, snow piled up on the ground, the woman listening to her could feel the warm air in Beaufort, hear the mewing of gulls, smell the magnolias and the jasmine, see the sharp-edged shiny greenness of palmettos, feel sand warm to the touch, see the great fireflies flitting about high up in the tops of the trees at night.

Harriet and her one-woman audience were no longer in a quiet kitchen in the North; they were in cypress swamps, or walking under live oaks hung with Spanish moss that waved like gray drapery overhead; they saw cotton fields and rice fields, and heard the swash of a river against the banks, and listened to the aching sweetness of a mockingbird, on an island where an incredible moon turned night into day.

Sometimes she went even farther back in her memory, to the days of the plantation and the overseer and the master. Then her listener could see a row of sway-backed cabins, smell the smoky smell from the fireplaces, could see a fifteen-year-old girl huddled under a dirty blanket, could see the great hole in her head and blood pouring from what should have been a mortal wound.

As she went farther and farther back in time, she spoke of the old slave ships, and the horror of the Middle Passage, retelling the stories she had heard as a child, stories of whips and chains and branding irons, of a quenchless thirst, and the black smell of death in the hold of a Yankee slaver. The word freedom became more than a word, it became a glory over everything.

Whoever heard her talk like that had a deeper understanding of the long hard way she had come, had a deeper understanding of what lay behind Gettysburg and Appomattox.

In 1903 she turned her home and twenty-five acres of land over to the African Methodist Episcopal Zion Church of Auburn, to be used as a home for the sick, the poor, the homeless, though she continued to live there herself. She wanted it called the John Brown Home. But shortly afterward, she expressed her dissatisfaction about the way the home was being conducted. The colored people in Auburn felt that they could not possibly support an institution which took its inmates in free of charge, and so began to charge an admittance fee.

Harriet, who to the end of her life retained that rarest of human virtues, compassion, said: "When I give the Home over to Zion Church, what do you suppose they did? Why, they made a rule that nobody should come in without a hundred dollars. Now I wanted to make a rule that nobody could come in unless they had no money. What's the good of a Home if a person who wants to get in has to have money?"

She died on March 10, 1913. Of her old friends and associates, only Sanborn and Higginson were still alive. The others had gone long before: Theodore Parker, Thomas Garrett, William H. Seward, William Lloyd Garrison, Frederick Douglass, Colonel James Montgomery.

In many ways she represented the end of an era, the most dramatic, and the most tragic, era in American history. Despite her work as a nurse, a scout, and a spy, in the Civil War, she will be remembered longest as a conductor on the Underground Railroad, the railroad to freedom—a short, indomitable woman, sustained by faith in a living God, inspired by the belief that freedom was a right all men should enjoy, leading bands of trembling fugitives out of Tidewater Maryland.

On July 12, 1914, the city of Auburn paid tribute to her. During the day flags were flown at half-mast. At night a tremendous mass meeting was held in the Auditorium, where a bronze tablet which had been inscribed to her memory was unveiled. The tablet was placed on the front entrance of the Courthouse in Auburn. This is what it says:

IN MEMORY OF HARRIET TUBMAN.
BORN A SLAVE IN MARYLAND ABOUT 1821.
DIED IN AUBURN, N.Y., MARCH 10TH, 1913.
CALLED THE MOSES OF HER PEOPLE,

DURING THE CIVIL WAR. WITH RARE
COURAGE SHE LED OVER THREE HUNDRED
NEGROES UP FROM SLAVERY TO FREEDOM,
AND RENDERED INVALUABLE SERVICE
AS NURSE AND SPY.
WITH IMPLICIT TRUST IN GOD
SHE BRAVED EVERY DANGER AND
OVERCAME EVERY OBSTACLE. WITHAL
SHE POSSESSED EXTRAORDINARY
FORESIGHT AND JUDGMENT SO THAT
SHE TRUTHFULLY SAID
"ON MY UNDERGROUND RAILROAD
I NEBBER RUN MY TRAIN OFF DE TRACK
AN' I NEBBER LOS' A PASSENGER."
THIS TABLET IS ERECTED
BY THE CITIZENS OF AUBURN.

Index

Index

Charlestown, Va., 192

Chase, John, 138, 144, 151

Chesapeake Bay, 1, 17-18, 22, 102

Choptank River, 8, 22, 92

Civil War, 201-11

Clay, Henry, 34, 44, 105

Clingman, Mr., of N.C., 93

Coffin, Levi, 195

Combahee River raid, 205-07

Compromise of 1820, 142

Compromise of 1850, 105

Confederate States of America (*see also* Civil War), 201-02

Congress, and slavery, 93, 105, 141

contrabands, 202-07, 209-10, 217

Cook, James, Mrs., 28-34, 65-66

Cornish, Samuel, 44

Craft, William and Ellen, 127-28

Curtis, George Ticknor, 115

Darby, Penn., 10

Davids, Tice, 47-49

Davis, Jefferson, 201

Davis, Nelson, 213-15

Declaration of Independence, 27

Douglas, Stephen, 140-41

Douglass, Frederick, 128, 132, 152, 178, 190-91, 220

Durrant, Henry K., 209-10

Eastern Shore, *see* Tidewater Maryland

emancipation of slaves, 204, 211

Fillmore, Millard, 111

Fortress Monroe, 210-11

Fort Sumter, 201

Framingham, Mass., 189

Freedom's Journal, 44

Fugitive Slave Law, 105, 106, 111, 113, 117, 122, 142, 178, 195, 202

Garrett, Sarah, 10

Garrett, Thomas, 10, 80-81, 124-25, 130, 150, 155, 163-64, 165, 175, 177, 183, 188, 199-200, 220

Garrison, William Lloyd, 63, 71-72, 105, 190, 220

Gilmore, General, 209

Grant, Ulysses S., General, 210-11

Greene, Harriet, 3-6, 9-10, 12, 16-18, 21-22, 28, 29, 31-33, 36-38, 45, 58, 61, 62, 65, 66, 74-75, 79, 91, 138, 143-44, 147-49, 168-78, 209, 211, 213

Hall, Judge, 80

Harper's Ferry, 191-92

Harriet, the Moses of Her People, 214

Harth, Mingo, 15

Henry, John Campbell, 151, 161

Higginson, Thomas Wentworth, 185, 189, 190, 204, 220

Hopkins, Samuel Miles, 214

Hughlett, William R., 156, 161

Hunn, John, 80

Hunter, David, General, 209

224

Index

ABOUT THE AUTHOR

ANN PETRY spent her childhood in Old Saybrook, Connecticut, where her family owned a drugstore. She herself was graduated from the College of Pharmacy at the University of Connecticut. After her marriage she lived in New York for ten years, but eventually moved back to her native state. *Harriet Tubman: Conductor on the Underground Railroad* reflects Mrs. Petry's special interest in slavery and her belief "that the majority of textbooks used in high schools do not give an adequate or accurate picture of the history of slavery in the United States." Mrs. Petry has also written *Tituba of Salem Village* for young readers.